D0065251

Thomas D. Clark
of Kentucky

Thomas D. Clark of Kentucky

An Uncommon Life in the Commonwealth

Edited by John E. Kleber

The University Press of Kentucky

Publication of this volume was made possible in part by a grant from the National Endowment for the Humanities.

Copyright © 2003 by The University Press of Kentucky

Scholarly publisher for the Commonwealth,
serving Bellarmine University, Berea College, Centre College of Kentucky,
Eastern Kentucky University, The Filson Historical Society, Georgetown College,
Kentucky Historical Society, Kentucky State University, Morehead State University,
Murray State University, Northern Kentucky University, Transylvania University,
University of Kentucky, University of Louisville, and Western Kentucky University.
All rights reserved.

Editorial and Sales Offices: The University Press of Kentucky
663 South Limestone Street, Lexington, Kentucky 40508 4008

Frontispiece: Dr. Thomas D. Clark in Estill County, October 23, 2002.
Photo by Charles Bertram/Lexington *Herald-Leader.*

08 07 06 05 04 03   5 4 3 2 1

Library of Congress Cataloging-in-Publication Data

 Thomas D. Clark of Kentucky : a uncommon life in the commonwealth / edited by John Kleber.
     p.   cm.
Includes bibliographical references and index.
   ISBN 0-8131-2297-X (alk. paper)
   1. Clark, Thomas Dionysius, 1903-   2. Historians—Kentucky—Biography.
3. Kentucky—Biography. 4. Kentucky—Historiography. I. Kleber, John E., 1941-
   E175.5.C56K46   2003
   976.9'007'202—dc21   2003007144

This book is printed on acid-free recycled paper meeting the requirements of the American National Standard for Permanence in Paper for Printed Library Materials.

∞ ✦

Manufactured in the United States of America.

Member of the Association of
American University Presses

Contents

Section photo credits

THE LIFE (page 1)

Thomas D. Clark, circa 1930

THE HISTORIAN (page 9)

Thomas D. Clark in his office at the University of Kentucky, circa 1955.

THE ADVOCATE (page 69)

Thomas D. Clark (foreground) at the Dedication of his papers to the University of Kentucky Library, Oct. 30, 1992. Bill Marshall (background), UK Special Collections.

THE FRIEND (page 143)

Joking after a group photo in front of Ashland. Left to right, Congressman Ernie Fletcher, Scotty Baesler, Thomas D. Clark, Larry Hopkins, and William P. Curlin Jr. November 12, 2002. Photo by Charles Bertram/Lexington Herald-Leader.

THE WORKS (page 217)

Dr. Thomas D. Clark looks over the outline for the large terrazzo map of Kentucky in the main lobby of the Kentucky History Center, under construction in February 1999. Photo by Lexington Herald-Leader.

Foreword

CARL N. DEGLER

When I was a beginning assistant professor at Vassar College on the banks of the Hudson River in New York, I tried as often as I could to visit historical conventions. There I could observe and occasionally meet the great names of the profession whose books or articles I had been reading and admiring. (I was bookish in those days.) I was especially excited at meetings of the Southern Historical Association, for the South was just gaining my attention as a region of the United States; it would soon become a long-term interest of mine. At those meetings I might try to gain the attention of one of the Greats in order to compliment his work. (At that time there were almost no women historians at those conventions, North or South.) The usual response from the author in question was pleasant and appreciative but little more. I was pleased at the encounter, nonetheless.

That is how I came to know Tom Clark. Instead, it was Tom, striding along a corridor at the convention hotel and seeing my name-tag who came right up to me in his vigorous way, saying, "I am glad to see you" as he warmly shook my hand. "Sarah Blanding told me a lot about you. You know," he continued, "she and I used to teach at Kentucky. She is a great gal." At that time Sarah Blanding was not only a native Kentuckian but the president of Vassar College, and Sarah's friendship with Tom was already helping me to obtain some travel money for the meetings of the Southern Historical Association.

(Of course, only much later could I call her, "Sarah.") Tom was one of those Greats, but I did not know that then. He was already a past president of the Southern Historical Association and also of the larger Organization of American Historians. When I first met him I had not yet read what became one of his characteristic studies of the rural South, his *Pills, Petticoats, and Plows: The Southern Country Store.* Only later as I moved more deeply into southern history did I draw upon his three-volume bibliography, *Travels in the Old South.*

To understand my friendship with Tom Clark you have to know that I was born and reared in New Jersey—in *northern* New Jersey, in fact. Some historians who have been born and reared in the South require some time to adjust to us northerners as we dig into the southern past. That was never true with Tom, partly, I suppose, because of my connection with Sarah Blanding, but more likely because he was not simply a regionalist. That identity was evident in his lecturing, studying and writing about aspects of the United States beyond the South. Southern rural history was undoubtedly Tom's first love, but he also spread that deep interest into the rural Middle West and the thinly populated frontier. Given his outlook and reputation beyond the South, it was hardly surprising that upon his retirement from Kentucky, Tom took up a prestigious visiting professorship at Indiana University, out of which emerged his three-volume history of that innovative educational institution, and which was published when he was only seventy-four.

Tom has a wonderful, strong voice and energetic manner that can be recognized from a distance. I never heard him lecture, I regret to say, but his public lectures at prestigious universities in the North and the South tell us much about his delivery and his professional reputation in the course of his century-long career. He was, as I say, a historian of rural America, yet despite that apparently limited interest, European universities at Vienna and Athens invited him to lecture.

It would be a mistake to push too hard on Tom's undeniable rural outlook, for again and again in the essays contained in this Festschrift you will find not only details of his works but also something of the variety of historical subjects he has discovered and pushed into the course of his century. He has continually spread his wings into new as well as old topics. Early on, for instance, he started writing economic history, detailing the history of an early southern railroad and, at another time, explaining the history of a branch of the Second Bank of the United States. He also delved into the history of journalism at one point, only to turn at another time to the native humor of frontier life. More recently he put together a study of Kentucky historical cartography. Somewhat later, in 1983, he dug into environmental history in a book he called *The Greening of the South.*

Most of that range of works and activities I simply did not know about when we used to chat from convention to convention. One of the reasons for my lack of information was that Tom never felt it necessary to talk about his latest book, article, or project, though they poured from the presses regularly. Our conversation usually confined itself to inquiries about what I was doing, and then maybe a remark about how Sarah Blanding was making out at Vassar, usually accompanied by an old story from Sarah's colorful life in their old days in Kentucky. With it always came that Tom Clark warmth and chuckle, and the twinkle in the eye.

What a century his life has been for all of us. Not only for Tom's surviving a centennial of such achievement and recognition, but especially for recognizing that new accomplishments and marks of recognition are still emerging from him. Or, put another way, it is good to be providing some measure of recognition of those achievements by and remembrances about Tom, for today he is able to read these remarks and remember us. So, dear reader, take a look below at these achievements and memories and enjoy.

Preface

JOHN E. KLEBER

Any life lived to age one hundred is worthy of recognition; when it is a life of magnificent accomplishments it must also be celebrated. Such is the life of Thomas Dionysius Clark, and this book is a part of that celebration.

Dr. Clark is my teacher, mentor, and friend. I was his student at the University of Kentucky shortly before he left there to go to Indiana University. Later, when I was teaching at Morehead State University, he prevailed upon me to edit *The Kentucky Encyclopedia*. Throughout that arduous task he was my inspiration and support. For forty years he has greeted me with warmth, amused me with wit, and plied me with letters pounded out on a typewriter that has worked nearly as long and hard as himself.

That said, it comes as no surprise that I was delighted to be asked by Stephen Wrinn, director of the University Press of Kentucky, to edit this Festschrift. With advice from James Klotter, I decided upon a topical approach that would look at the life of Thomas D. Clark as historian, advocate, and friend. The essayists were chosen based on their knowledge of Clark, and each was asked to write from a personal perspective. I am aware that others might have done likewise, and many wished to do so. Unfortunately the constraints of time and space limited it to those sixteen people. Doubtless those others would have reiterated what is said here, and so these authors speak for many when praising Clark's long life.

"Thank God for Mississippi" has been a frequently spoken adage bemoaning some failure of Kentucky—at one time its educational system. It was comforting to know that we were not last in everything. Yet the words have a refreshingly positive meaning when we can be thankful that Mississippi gave us Tom Clark. From the moment he detrained at the Lexington depot in 1928 to the present, he has made contributions to his adopted state that have helped to raise it in rankings. "For age is opportunity no less than youth," noted Longfellow. Clark has never missed an opportunity to change things and touch lives, whether as historian, advocate, or friend. Each chapter here is written by someone whose life was touched, as was mine, and who had the opportunity to see the changes wrought by this scion of the Magnolia state. To read their words is to thank providence as well for giving Thomas D. Clark longevity.

I hope this book will do more than celebrate that life. May it document deeds done and inspire others to emulate them. May it recall for Clark the words of Walt Whitman: "So here I sit in the early candle-light of old age—I and my book—casting backward glances over our travel'd road." If I know Tom Clark, and I do, chances are he won't be looking backward long but will be looking ahead to the next book to be written, to the special cause to be advocated, to the new friend to be met.

PART I. THE LIFE

Biography

WALTER A. BAKER

Tom Clark once said, "I have known every Kentucky governor since Isaac Shelby." While this literally is not so, he is undoubtedly more knowledgeable about Kentucky—its history, its leaders, and its people—than any other person. For more than a half century each of Kentucky's governors has sought Clark's counsel on how our state can avoid repeating the mistakes of its past and insure progress for its future.

Yet Kentucky's best-known historian is not a native Kentuckian. Born in Louisville, Mississippi, on July 14, 1903, Tom Clark is the son of a Mississippi cotton farmer and a public school teacher. His father's family had its origins in Virginia; his mother's in Charleston, South Carolina. The eldest of six children, following the seventh grade he worked for two years full-time on a farm. This was followed by work at a sawmill, then as a cabin boy and deckhand on a dredge boat. Finally, at the age of eighteen he entered Choctaw County Agricultural High School. By 1925 he had his high school diploma and with savings from a ten-acre cotton crop enrolled at the University of Mississippi.

In 1990 the Kentucky General Assembly honored Clark by declaring him to be Kentucky's Historian Laureate. In an honors convocation in the Capitol Rotunda Governor Brereton Jones described Clark as "Kentucky's greatest treasure."

Clark has a lengthy influence on the Department of History at the University of Kentucky, but he has also influenced the study of Kentucky history at other Kentucky institutions. In his mid-nineties he decided to place his collection of Kentucky history volumes in a college library. Believing that its impact would be minimal at the University of Kentucky, he donated the entire collection to Lindsey Wilson College in Columbia, Kentucky, where the college expanded its Holloway Library to add a Thomas D. Clark Room to house this collection.

It is ironic that Clark, who has been the premier figure in recording Kentucky history, has never been afforded the honor of serving as president of the Kentucky Historical Society. Long a member and participant in KHS activities, Clark was nominated in 1959 to serve as president. But because of a dispute over a matter pertaining to the relationship of the city of Frankfort and the Society, KHS members from Frankfort organized a write-in campaign that saw Willard R. Jillson defeat Clark by one vote.

People are always amazed at the energy and stamina of Clark, who has long since outlived his contemporaries. A few years ago Murray State University wanted to honor him. They issued an invitation for him to come to an honors convocation and offered to send a car and driver to bring him to Western Kentucky from his home in Lexington. Clark refused the offer, saying he would just swing by himself, as he was driving to Mississippi to visit his two sisters.

While historians analyze the past, Tom Clark has always been interested in the future. UK President Lee Todd Jr. tells the story of a luncheon meeting to which he was invited by Earl Wallace, conservationist and preservationist, where Todd met Clark. The two older men were talking about Kentucky. Wallace asked, "Why are two old men worried about Kentucky?" Clark responded, "I guess because we still think we can do something about it." Virginia Fox, former head of Kentucky Educational Television, describes Clark as "a pragmatic idealist and, above all, a harbinger of hope."

Clark's coming to Kentucky was a fortuitous blessing, which, but for fate, might never have occurred. Offered fellowships at both the University of Cincinnati and UK, Clark says that he flipped a nickel and the decision came up for Kentucky. He came to Kentucky "for a degree and saw his first Republican." Gaining his master's degree in 1929, he left for Duke University to work on a doctorate, which he received in 1932. Clark returned to the University of Kentucky in 1931 to complete his dissertation. There, employed by Dr. Frank L. McVey, he experienced the financial woes that struck public higher education in the Great Depression. The Kentucky legislature cut funds, and Clark wound up with only $1,100 of the $1,800 promised by McVey.

Clark's career at the University of Kentucky spanned the period 1931 through 1968. He became chairman of the History Department in 1942 and held that position until 1965. Thousands of students attended Clark's classes during his UK years. Many Kentuckians who went on to positions of leadership in the state first learned of Kentucky's past through Clark's lectures. Among those were Edward T. Breathitt, later governor, and John Ed Pearce, longtime *Courier-Journal* writer and editorialist.

Although most think of Clark solely as a professor at the University of Kentucky, such is not the entire story. Through his career he also taught, among other places, at Harvard, Duke, North Carolina, Tennessee, Rochester, Chicago, Wyoming, Wisconsin, Kent State, Stanford, and Indiana. Overseas he lectured at Oxford as well as in Greece, Yugoslavia, and India. After retirement he taught for six years at Indiana University and three years at Eastern Kentucky University, as well as periods at Wisconsin and Winthrop College in Rock Hill, South Carolina. Indiana University awarded Clark an honorary degree and named him a Professor Emeritus.

If Tom Clark was popular as a lecturer, he was equally diligent as a researcher and writer. His *History of Kentucky*, published in 1937, remains six decades later one of the standard works on this state. But Clark achieved distinction as a historian in many areas: state history, southern history, frontier history, and institutional history.

Besides his *History of Kentucky*, Clark also published many works, including *History of Clark County*; *History of Laurel County*; *The Kentucky*; *Kentucky: Land of Contrast*; and *Agrarian Kentucky*. At age 99 he coauthored *The People's House: Governor's Mansions of Kentucky*.

The study of Kentucky as a frontier whetted Clark's appetite for the frontier period in American history, resulting in *The Rampaging Frontier* in 1939 and thirty-six years later in *The Great American Frontier*.

In regional and southern history Clark was chief editor of two massive multivolume publications: *Travels in the Old South* and *Travels in the New South*. Additional works in this area include *The Beginnings of the L & N: A Pioneer Southern Railroad*; *Pills, Petticoats, and Plows*; *The Rural Papers and the New South*; and *The Southern Country Editor*.

The invitation of former Kentucky Law School dean Elvis J. Stahr, then president of Indiana University, for Clark to come to Indiana following his retirement at Kentucky resulted in Clark's producing a four-volume history of the Indiana institution.

Among his peers Clark has demonstrated national leadership. In 1947 he was president of the Southern Historical Association. From 1948 to 1952 he was editor of the *Journal of Southern History*. In 1957 he became president of the Organization of American Historians, and he chaired its executive committee 1957-63.

As father of the Special Collections and Archives at the University of Kentucky, Clark roamed the state and region rescuing priceless documents and papers from decay and destruction. After learning of a truck loaded with precious archival materials leaving a warehouse in Frankfort for destruction, he appealed to Governor A.B. Chandler, who ordered the materials delivered to Clark.

Two major state facilities have resulted from Clark's vision and his effectiveness in transforming vision into reality. The first is the Kentucky Library and Archives Building, erected in Frankfort in the late 1970s. The second, the crown jewel of Kentucky history, is the $29 million Kentucky History Center in downtown Frankfort. During the 1994 General Assembly Clark teamed with Libby Jones, wife of Governor Jones, and they became one of the most effective lobbying teams working to secure legislative approval and funding for the Kentucky History Center. Clark and Kentucky's first lady took legislators on guided tours of an old bourbon whiskey warehouse then being used to house part of the Kentucky Historical Society collection. After demonstrating the danger to priceless artifacts, they then delivered a most persuasive sales talk over food and beverages at the governor's mansion. Few legislators could resist the charm and persuasiveness of this team. The appropriation was approved and construction began on the Kentucky History Center. The library in the Kentucky History Center is the Thomas D. Clark Library and a large bas-relief of Clark, by sculptor Ed Hamilton, welcomes visitors into the magnificent hall of the center.

Just as he preserved for others the basic resources for research, Clark in 1943 helped establish the University of Kentucky Press. Two decades later he participated in the founding of the University Press of Kentucky, a statewide consortium that includes most of Kentucky's regional and research universities and private colleges.

Family has always been a priority for Clark. At Duke he met Martha Elizabeth Turner, whom he married in 1933. This marriage lasted sixty-two years, until Beth's death in 1995. He and Beth had two children: Thomas Bennett Clark, a Lexington lawyer, and Ruth Elizabeth Stone, wife of a Western Kentucky University history professor. A year and a half after Beth's death he married Loretta Brock.

Professor, historian, editor, lecturer, author—all describe Thomas D. Clark's life and activities. But statesman best portrays the role he has played across the commonwealth of Kentucky during his retirement years. He has been a leading advocate for better education, preservation of history and the environment, and progressive constitutional change. Al Smith, host of Kentucky Educational Television's *Comment on Kentucky*, labels Clark "our greatest living citizen."

Each year at the first meeting of the Leadership Kentucky class, Tom Clark is the person asked to discuss Kentucky's past and to pose goals for Kentucky's future. Whether among students, community leaders, or seasoned political operatives, Clark is respected for his calm but stern reflections on Kentucky's past shortcomings and his admonitions for the future. As former Governor Edward Breathitt relates, "Tom Clark is a Kentucky treasure. He probably has more credibility than any other Kentuckian in the field of history, public affairs, and political reform."

PART II. THE HISTORIAN

Kentucky Historian

JAMES C. KLOTTER

In 1941, John F. "Sunny" Day's book *Bloody Ground* appeared. In it
the journalist gave his impressions of Appalachian Kentucky. Chapter 12 told of going to a "funeralizing" on Troublesome Creek. Day
had another person with him as he made his way up Betty Branch of
Troublesome, someone who was also using the trip to gather information for a book. Journalist Day began his eventual chapter with
"Tom" picking up a piece of shale and skipping it across the narrow
creek, then remarking, "Looks just like any other branch in the hills,
doesn't it?"

"Yeh," Day answered.

Tom noted, "With such a euphonious name, seems somehow like
it ought to be different."

They talked of the deaths along those waters and walked on. Day
wrote later of his traveling companion: "Tom is a university professor, but I found out long ago his profession shouldn't be held against
him. Good old easy-spoken Tom from the Mississippi mud flats, he's
got more energy and horse sense than half a dozen ordinary college
professors." Day explained that Tom had written three books about
Kentucky and now was working on his fourth.

The university professor had taught a young girl in his class who
lived in the area, and Emma—"willowy, fair, and keen-eyed"—now
served as the only instructor of a one-room school. She and her sister

guided them on their eight-mile trek to the memorial service in the mountains.

As they walked, Tom commented that "Those confound locusts make a lot of noise, don't they?" Meanwhile his shoes got muddier and muddier as he crossed and re-crossed the creek that served as their road. Then, just as Tom noted that it looked like rain, a truck picked them up and took them to the graveyard for the delayed funeral.

There they heard over three hours of hell and brimstone preaching from a series of voices, all intent on helping hardened sinners see the errors of their ways before death overtook them too. Finally, "Sunny" Day and Tom drifted outside to listen to the conversations of those around them. Then their day ended and they moved on.[1]

"Tom" was of course Thomas D. Clark, then professor of history at the University of Kentucky, in Lexington. He had firsthand knowledge of the possible response to newpaperman Day's stories, for after an initial one appeared in the local press, an angry student from Breathitt County had stormed in Clark's office, declaring that the newspaper story had many errors. The young man contended, for example, that an old log cabin shown in the piece was not even in his home county. Clark wrote later, "By pure coincidence I knew that the old Hudson Cabin was indeed located just inside Breathitt. . . , a fact that completely flabbergasted the student." He said of that journey with Day: "We slept in the same mountain beds, ate a lot of greasy food, got a car stuck in bottomless mountain creek mud, and viewed human activities." Clark also attended a "Holy Roller" religious meeting, walked with a "revenooer" as he raided a moonshine still, and visited a Hard-Shell Baptist footwashing, where he and Day made the mistake of sitting on the women's side of the church before a deacon revealed to them the error of their ways.[2] Then, like Day, Clark returned to the Bluegrass to write his own book.

That trip reveals much about Tom Clark, the writer of state history, and about the man himself. First of all, he stands as a son of the soil. He skipped stones across creeks; he listened to the locust; he saw the signs of rain in the sky; he walked the muddy roads. His world would not be one restricted to dusty tomes in dark libraries, or quiet halls in placid academe. Clark would be in all those places and would learn from them, but he also learned the lessons from the wider world, from the sources of the soil. The result would be better informed, more readable prose, and that would translate into books that brought history to a wider audience. Such treks liberated his writing from the restrictive tones of academic prose, even while he held true to its tenets.

Those trips to places distant from ivy-covered walls may also have been good for the ego. Clark recalls how he once rushed from his classroom to travel to a small county. He expected to present one of his fairly standard talks to a sparse group. Once he got there, however, Clark found a huge crowd waiting. Mentally primed by that, he started thinking how he could make the talk more special for them since they had made the effort to come out and hear him. As he got up to speak, his excitement rapidly faded when a man whispered to him, "Now Doc, don't speak too long. These people are here waitin' for the hog auction to begin." Tom Clark seldom played second fiddle to a hog auction in his life, however.

On a second front, while Day's comment about "soft-spoken Tom" might be questioned by those who later received needed criticism from Clark on key points, Day's description of Clark's energy and horse sense would be challenged by few. Those characterizations would hold true for all his life.

A third matter that comes through clearly in the trip to Troublesome concerns Thomas D. Clark's connection to people. A former student guides them on their odyssey, and the professor has kept up with her after classes ended. He talks to people outside the memorial service, at a religious gathering, and on a moonshine raid. Tom meets the individuals of Kentucky and they become flesh and blood personalities, not cardboard caricatures on his pages. A richer and fuller history results.

An example of how all that unfolds in the pages of a book emerges in Clark's own chapter 12 in *The Kentucky*, which appeared a year after Day's work. In his chapter entitled "Funeralizing," the historian writes about the practice of delayed funerals, planned a year in advance. He tells of grave houses and folk legends, of the songs sung by those sitting on rough log benches, of preachers paying respect to the dead while trying to "convert the living and to warm over the converts who have grown cold." The professor/observer writes of how a minister first offers "the hackneyed excuse that he is not prepared . . . but it is imperious duty that has called him, and the Lord, he hopes, will blaze the way. Soon, he is positive, . . . he will be able to warm up to a sermon." Clark tells of how the preacher breathlessly grows stronger and how "a loud Amen tells him he is rising 'higher and higher.'" Finally, "a loud handclap is an invitation to let go with all his might." Readers can easily visualize the scene and the emotion present.[3]

In *The Kentucky*, Clark alternates between chapters on historical happenings and personalities, and more current ones, such as the "Funeralizing" chapter. He mixes folk humor tales with hard historical analysis. For example, in writing of "Hard-Shell" Baptists, he tells how some people wonder what kind of preacher a sleeping minister is. The man is dressed well—perhaps a Presbyterian?— but his denomination seems unclear. So they examine his saddlebags, and find a bottle of Kentucky's finest. A woman holds up the evidence and proclaims, "Oh, he's an old Hard-Shell Baptist! Here is his bottle of whisky!"[4]

Yet at the end of his "Funeralizing" chapter, Clark also concludes: "The storm has passed, and the dead have been served. Everyday life takes up again. . . . Rural isolated America is enjoying the thing for which it hungers—company and a crowd. . . . Grief for the departed one is genuine, but so is the interest in the company and friendly communion of the neighbors." There, in an understanding tone, he explains that the Primitive Regular Baptist Church "was the one religious faith which could accept realistically the primeval limitations of the country at the head of Kentucky hills and succeed in living with a degree of happiness."[5] And so his research trip became the reality in his book of history.

From the time he arrived in the commonwealth in 1928, as a twenty-five-year-old, Clark remembers, "I became interested in Kentucky's history right off and I have never lost that interest." That concern has benefited the state in many ways over the years, whether in building research collections, producing reference works, writing history, or just making Kentucky a better place for the future.[6]

Yet, while the general public of the state deeply appreciates such efforts and honors him for all that, not all give the prophet honor in his own country. As Clark notes, "an intellectual misfortune of the present era" has been the widening gap between professional historians and interested others who write history. While many validly criticize some of that writing by nonprofessionals for its lack of perspective, interpretation, and criticism, sometimes those views spill over into disparagement of professional historians like Clark who choose to write on state subjects.[7]

The Mississippian turned Kentuckian finds such appraisals ridiculous: "There are historians who say state history has no significance and is clearly a local anecdotal thing. That is wrong, wrong, wrong. That is where . . . the people live." Moreover, he intones, historians have an obligation to more than just other followers of Clio—"not to dig up corpses and expose them to other historians and then bury them. I think history should have some fundamental meaning, not only to the profession itself . . . but to society in general."[8]

Clark understood early that writing the history of a state or region was nothing less than looking at the nation's history writ small: "Grassroots research," he stressed, ". . . builds a very solid foundation to broader research projects." No matter what level is under study, the same issues arise: Why do things occur? What explains them? What does that mean for us today, and in the future? As the Historian Laureate for Life acknowledged, "I spend a lot of time trying to sort out the realities of Kentucky from the romantic concepts." Once that was accomplished, he could turn to studying the "cadence of life itself," the value systems, the institutions, the sense of place, and all the things that make an entity a whole. Out of such work, others can combine the various stories and present a truly national view.[9]

In area after area, Clark's own efforts show the enduring value of such study and the benefits from it, now and for the future. He began his work when few sizeable research collections existed in the state and when the diligent researcher had to go almost door to door to locate possible materials. Clark has helped change all that (as noted elsewhere in this book). At the University of Kentucky Special Collections, at the State Archives, and at the Kentucky History Center, he either initiated or aided in endeavors to make research materials more easily available for those who come after him seeking to mark out their own research contributions. A futurist wrote that "We must love our grandchildren more than we love ourselves." Clark has paved the way for his historical grandchildren to follow.[10]

Clark has also vastly simplified historical research for future generations by his editorial work in reference books on Kentucky. Some of those may be limited in scope. His *Footloose in Jacksonian America*, for example, presented the 1829–30 and 1836 travel diaries of Robert W. Scott of Franklin County, followed by an excellent eighty-page life of Scott and his agrarian world. More expansive coverage came from his efforts as one of three associate editors of *The Kentucky Encyclopedia* and *The Encyclopedia of Louisville*. In addition to giving advice on subjects and authors for inclusion, he also read the submissions to check for errors and produced numerous entries himself, on a variety of topics. In just the entries for the letters "A" and "B" in *The Kentucky Encyclopedia*, for instance, he wrote about almanacs, Bee Rock (cliffs on the Rockcastle River), the Bill of Rights, Black Jack Corner (a jog in the state boundary line), the *Blair* v. *Williams* court case, the Book Thieves (a collectors' group in Lexington), boundaries, and Edwin Bryant (author and editor). Clark also penned the excellent fifteen-page historical overview to that volume.[11]

Besides his work in the collecting and reference fields, Thomas D. Clark has shared his knowledge of the state through his writing, and for that he is perhaps best known. The poet wrote that "Of all those arts in which the wise excel / Nature's chief masterpiece is writing well."[12] Clark has used the gift of the gods exceedingly wisely and well, both in books with more specific themes, and in general histories. The result is that those who read his work and walk down his historical roads with him usually find it a very satisfying trip.

Clark's research into state history has resulted not only in numerous works dealing with Kentucky specifically but has also helped inform his many other works on western and southern history. In 1939, for instance, in his *Rampaging Frontier*, he told of the First West that was Kentucky and quoted a Virginian on the character of the people in this new land. When a person had left the Old Dominion, people said, "He has gone to hell or Kentucky." Such illustrations brought Clark's summation: "The West was a free land: free with morals, free with conversation, free with swearing, free with strangers, and free with the Lord."[13]

Similarly, when writing about various facets of the South, Clark has used his state research to add to the story being presented. In *Pills,*

Petticoats, and Plows: The Southern Country Store (1944), Mississippi's greatest export to Kentucky tells of the fashions sold in those places: "Pictures of Kentucky politicians of the nineties make the average state legislator appear to be an escaped inmate from the county jail." Four years later, when presenting the history of southern country editors, he quoted an 1870 *Breckinridge News* editorial on U.S. Senator John S. Williams: "An ambitious frog swells with self-conceit until it imagines itself an ox. General Williams is the ambitious and conceited frog of the Kentucky politics." More than three decades later, when portraying *The Greening of the South*, the agrarian related how one Kentucky land company had cut all its timber by 1921: "Their mills stood idle and abandoned, railroad trackage fell into disrepair and decay, logging equipment rusted at the spot where it loaded the last logs." Such word pictures allow readers to understand better the points the historian makes about the South, in change and unchanging.[14]

But most of all, Tom Clark has used his research into the mind and culture of Kentuckians to bang out on his battered typewriter a series of books that have defined the study of the state's history. He has created images and interpretations that have become standard fare for how Kentucky has been described, decade after decade.

Some of those studies may be more limited in scope but are still broad in vision. In articles, for example, on Kentucky's trade to the South, in hemp, livestock, and slaves, and on education in the commonwealth generally, he has broadened the historical writing on those topics. In particular, his 1985 *Register of the Kentucky Historical Society* article "Kentucky Education through Two Centuries of Political and Social Change" painted a telling word picture of pedagogical failure, relieved only occasionally by successes to be remembered. Given first at the Shakertown Roundtable and then printed, his survey came four years before courts declared the state's whole educational system a failure. His cry about "the shameful wastage of precious and potential human creative talent" reached willing ears.[15] That mix of academic study and public advocacy showed the effect a historian can have on the larger community.

Less policy-oriented, but covering topics needing further historical study, were such Clark works as *Agrarian Kentucky* (1977) and *Historic Maps of Kentucky* (1979). In the first of those, the man who had grown up in the rural South often lovingly told of that world's strengths while at the same time criticizing the failures and problems that grew out of that agrarian soil. One of the concise volumes in the successful Bicentennial Bookshelf Series, *Agrarian Kentucky* stressed how the land left its impress on the people and prompted a provincialism "which gives spiritual essence to the commonwealth itself." Yet Clark also found fault with the inequities, sectionalism, nostalgia, and isolationism that made "cultural captives" of the people. While not the full history of Kentucky agriculture that Clark feels still needs to be written, the book provided an important start.[16]

While seemingly a vehicle to reprint early maps of Kentucky and to discuss other cartographic efforts, *Historic Maps of Kentucky* became much more. In some sixty pages of accompanying text, Clark focused new historical light on a dimly studied subject, the boundaries of the state. He told how surveyors marked those artificial lines, then he delved into the murky history of the Ohio River controversy, examined the Jackson Purchase, and closed with a discussion of the maps themselves. The book remains the best study of the subject and shows how diligent research and good writing can give historical life to the seemingly dullest of subjects.[17]

In spite of Thomas D. Clark's major contributions to Kentucky history in all those areas—collecting, reference sources, articles, limited-focus books—his chief efforts to tell the full state story lie in three works: *A History of Kentucky*, *The Kentucky*, and *Kentucky: Land of Contrast*. While each differs in its approach to the study of the state, together they give a full and often fresh view of the commonwealth's past, present condition, and possible future. Combined, they represent Thomas D. Clark's fullest scholarly contribution to Kentucky history.

"We needed a textbook," Clark recalled later. So he wrote one. Some one-volume surveys could be found for pre-college classes, and a few multivolume scholarly histories had appeared, but a good, professional one-volume work suitable for use in universities or in the homes of interested others simply did not exist. The raw data available in the half-century-old Collins *History,* and the good historical analysis and research present in the two volumes of text by William E. Connelley and E. Merton Coulter offered materials for a promising start, but the paucity of scholarly writing on many aspects of Kentucky usually meant that the thirty-four-year-old Clark had to do much of the original research himself.[18]

The result would be the 700-page *History of Kentucky* (1937), which became the standard text for the next six decades and which remains in print today. Intended "as a tool by which book the student and general reader are led into a broader field of study," it did just that. Starting with geography and then going into a chapter on resources, people, and the land, the book next looks at the movement west into the area and the period of European-American settlement. One of the most readable chapters follows, on frontier society. Then Clark resumes his analysis of chronological periods—statehood, the time to the Louisiana Purchase, the 1800–15 era, and the Old Court–New Court struggle. Next he takes the reader through various topical chapters dealing with early agriculture and industry; rivers, roads, and railroads; slavery; early education; the press (pre–Civil War and postwar); and culture (including architecture, artists, silversmiths, sculptors, writers, historians, and musicians), with a concluding part of that chapter on "The Kentucky Personality."[19]

Returning to the chronological arrangement, Clark then focuses on antebellum politics, the new constitution of 1850, and the Civil War. Once more he turns to education, economics, and "social responsibilities" in various places, then examines the politically turbulent 1890s and the assassination of a governor. His 1960 revision of the book includes a chapter on "Kentucky in Change," which emphasizes post–World War II trends in population, economics, race, roads, and politics. Though containing no notes, the book does include a bibliography and an appendix listing the governors of the state.

Positive reviews greeted the book, college classes have used it for seemingly eons, and it quickly shaped historians' interpretations. Like any pathbreaking work, it became the target for revisionists and, at the same time, the stimulus for hosts of new studies on Kentucky. When published, it represented the "cutting edge" of historical writing, and long remained the state standard.

Viewed from the perspective of the twenty-first century, *A History of Kentucky* has held up well, with some exceptions. Like other works of that era, it gives scant attention to Indians, and if they do appear they tend to be presented as "savages of the forest." Its views of women and of Reconstruction represent older interpretations. Throughout, more attention is given to pre–Civil War matters than to those since that conflict. The 1960 edition, for example, devotes 330 of its 460 pages of text to the time before 1865. Revisions tended to add information rather than change what had been written previously.[20]

Yet those matters pale in comparison to what the historian in his thirties accomplished. Throughout, the work reflects research in a wide variety of subjects. Solid, informed judgments mark virtually every page. So too does good writing. While textbooks impose certain restrictions on an author's prose, Clark still could enliven his narrative to keep the reader's interest. When writing about newspaperman George Prentice of the *Louisville Journal* and Prentice's feud with a rival editor, for instance, Clark notes how Prentice had gotten hold of an old Louisiana newspaper that told of a sensational murder. The editor pressed the paper to make it appear new, then had it sent anonymously to his rival with a note that it had been delivered by the packet *Waucousta,* which had just made the fastest passage on record from New Orleans. In fact, that ship, wrote Clark, "was such a leaky old craft that its crew was afraid to leave the bank in it." Prentice's rival took the bait, printed the old story as new, and even congratulated the *Waucousta* for its record trip. A delighted Prentice exposed it all and thereafter would taunt his rival when that person broke what seemed a sensational story, with the words: "Did that come by the *Waucousta?*"[21]

Inclusion of such stories not only entertains, but also gives readers insight into Prentice's wit and personality as well as the journalistic ethics and business practices of the era. In short, people learn more than had the story not been included. Clark also can use the sharp remark to make an important point, not just about the matter under discussion but about future policy. Long a critic of the state's outdated fourth constitution, he writes about the third constitution and how much difficulty people had in changing it, concluding that "for some unknown reason the commonwealth's citizens have felt that calling a constitutional convention was akin to disloyalty to established government."[22]

In short, *A History of Kentucky* when it appeared in 1937 represented a striking achievement by a still-young professor in a still-emerging profession. It showed excellent research—especially given the poor state of archival materials—good writing, coverage of diverse topics, and the author's wide breadth of knowledge of Kentucky history. Criticisms of it may remind us that no book is perfect, but they do little to diminish the overriding fact that Clark's *History* became the starting place for those who wanted to study the state's past, and long remained in that seminal position. When the authors of a new history of Kentucky completed their book sixty years after Clark's appeared, they dedicated it to Thomas D. Clark, for they knew that historians of the commonwealth's past must follow the historical trails he had blazed. They may make their own new scholarly paths, but they still start with him. Clark's *History* has endured, and justly so.[23]

Just four years later—and after writing a volume on Kentucky for young readers in between—Thomas D. Clark penned another book that included much state history, but from a very different perspective and approach. In 1942, *The Kentucky* appeared as a volume in the Rivers of America series. Its author would be the first historian asked to prepare a volume for this series, which usually featured more "popular" writers. The publishers obviously knew a good writer when they saw one, however, historian or not. Clark would say later, "I always felt that history was a living thing. It tells you so much about what you did and didn't do." In *The Kentucky*, that history lived.[24]

While obviously not a full history of the entire state, since it focuses only on the area drained by the Kentucky River, the book instead uses a series of historical and current vignettes to tell the story of that water course and the people who have lived in or near it. Some chapters include historical information only; others start with a story from the past, then move to a present-day feature; some use only recent information and observations. But whatever the approach, the format unshackled Clark from the constraints of chronology and from the textbook duty to cover certain facts. In his first chapter, on the river, Clark concludes by calling it "a thing of beauty and strength, but like Samson's Delilah, treacherous. Its story is varied, but never dull." *The Kentucky* itself presents a varied story, but never a dull one.[25]

The topics Clark covers range from Swift's Silver Mine to Shakers, from the thoroughbred race horse Lexington to the standardbred Nancy Hanks, from steamboats to Sally Ward, the famous belle, from Morgan's Raiders to Moonshiners, from foodways to "funeralizing," from Boonesborough to "Hard-Shell" Baptists. Readers learn about knaves (such as James Wilkinson), inventors, dreamers, singers, architects, resort owners, and even cockfighters. Clark tells about the whole range of the river, from the mountains to the Ohio, with reviews on each region. Of the Bluegrass, for example, he concludes that it is "more than a region which can be definitely located by a geologist or a geographer upon a soulless map. . . . It is likewise a state of mind, a matter of great community pride, and, so far as a region can be, a satisfactory way of life."[26]

Those words were in print in 1942 when the book originally came out. A half-century later a new edition appeared, and in it Tom Clark added a new chapter, one that revealed both the wordsmith and the influencer of public policy at his best. The man who had walked those river banks many times criticized the chemical pollution and the coal silt filling its basin. He also censured others: "All along the river and its myriad laterals human beings have mowed down the forests, spewed poisonous chemicals into streams, discharged cesspools and sewers over its banks, and festooned its shores with plastic jugs and every piece of waste human denizen had strength and will power enough to haul away from their overlittered premises. In due seasons the river has fought back." He tells of floods, of the increasing need by cities for more water, and of the deaths of communities along the river. Clark ends, however, by reminding readers that "The Kentucky flows on. . . . Like a wily gambler aboard one of the ancient Kentucky River steamboats, the stream holds all the aces and waits to play them at the moment when the human players have bet the water supply for a third of the Commonwealth's population." Tom Clark has continued to tell well the story of the river, its people, and its places.[27]

To some observers, Thomas D. Clark's *Kentucky: Land of Contrast* may be the best of his general state histories. Published in 1968—over a quarter of a century after *The Kentucky* and three decades after *A History of Kentucky*—it combines the strengths of both. It reveals the work of a much more mature scholar, one who has added information from additional years of research and who can offer more perspective for his judgments. In that sense, it reflects the scholarly strengths of Clark's *History*. On the other hand, its organization harkens back more to the Rivers of America series, and that results in a more readable tome than the *History*.

A volume in the Regions of America series, *Kentucky: Land of Contrast* is packed with good characterizations, fine writing, solid research, and frank conclusions. In the Preface, for example, the author makes his themes clear early. Of Kentucky he writes: "Its people have been isolated by geography, provincial at all times, and submissive to political influences which oftentimes have handicapped them in broadening their views of the world." Over the years, Clark notes, "The unyielding rock of agrarianism has shattered campaigns to revise the old ways of life." Complacent, tied to the past, Clark's Kentuckians of 1968 faced a future of vast change. That, however, only echoed the land they lived in: "It would be difficult to imagine a people embraced by a single set of political boundaries who presented sharper contrasts than have Kentuckians." The state truly could be called a land of contrast.[28]

Clark presents the many sides of Kentucky in his some three hundred pages of text through both topical and chronological chapters. After starting off with material on the early explorers, Boone, and the founding of the state, Clark offers some pungent comments about what he calls "one of the most unsatisfactory land claim and survey systems in North America," noting that the resulting documents "read more nearly like botanical inventories of Kentucky's virgin forests than as foundations for legal instruments." Chapters followed on river, religion, roads, and race relations, as well as on travelers' accounts, the "Athens of the West," and the "Mother of the West" (on those who left). Post–Civil War topics include looks at horse racing, bourbon, feuds, literature, Appalachia, and, of course, politics.[29]

Clark finds little to praise in the half-century of politics following the Brothers' War. In one place he says that leadership failed in that era "because a baggy-pants political control throttled everything that even smelled of progress. . . . A wave of conservatism and fear swept the state." Later, Clark faults flowery orators "who showered their moldy encomiums upon fair womanhood . . . and proclaimed the glories of the past whenever they could. . . . These windy scions rested their empty head figuratively on the bosom of fair Kentucky with gestures as monstrous as was their insincerity." Finally, he repeats one governor's comments that "there were two things he never wanted to have again. One was gonorrhea, and the other the governorship of Kentucky." Clark the critic constantly reminds the state that it can do—should do—better for itself if it truly wants a more promising future.[30]

Yet, even as he stressed the problems of the past, Clark also noted that the emerging presence of what was becoming a new Kentucky had its own dangers as well. His last sentence in the book warned: "The old individualism is being replaced by a rather blank kind of social and communal conformity, and the spirit of what was once a hardheaded old agrarian state is rapidly falling into a pattern of national sameness." That is vintage Tom Clark—reject parts of the past but remember that not all that is new is good, and accept change but do not forget the strengths of the state's history.[31]

In fact, all three of these major books on Kentucky show the elements that characterize Thomas D. Clark's work. He once indicated that "Writing is a lonely business, but I have from the start determined that what I wrote was going to have some style."[32] In that he succeeded. Readable prose characterizes Clark's writing on Kentucky history.

Another component of his craft, present throughout, is Tom

Clark's clear historical judgments. Few readers would not know how author Clark stands on a subject. Not afraid to commit himself in his conclusions, he gives his best interpretation, his fullest historical analysis, because that should be the role of the expert on the subject.

A third characteristic of Clark's Kentucky history writing concerns his versatility. He covers a wide range of topics, uses a variety of sources, and presents different approaches to the subjects.

And, finally, as a fourth element of his work, Clark constantly seeks to show the importance of history: "You have got to have some knowledge of the past to function in a society," he once declared. Without precedents, Clark asked, where would the court system be? Without personal history, how could the medical profession operate? And on and on. Clark sees the understanding of the past as a crucial factor in good citizenship and sound decision-making, and he stresses that belief over and over through his words and his actions.[33]

On November 12, 1994, ninety-one-year-old Tom Clark made still another trip into the Kentucky mountains, as he had done with John F. Day well over a half-century before. With him this time was the Executive Director of the Kentucky Historical Society, a then–forty-seven-year-old whom he called "Young Jim Klotter." They did not seek to gather information for a book, as before, but rather to dedicate a historical highway marker honoring the life of former Governor Bert Combs.

The travelers got to Manchester in Clay County in time for lunch. Dr. Clark indicated that he knew a good if out-of-the-way restaurant there. Arriving—finally, for it was *way* out-of-the-way—the two noted the sign outside: "Locals Eat Here." After a good meal, as they went to pay, Klotter suddenly noticed that Clark had seemingly disappeared. That was not good. Possible headlines flashed before his eyes—"Klotter loses Clark!" But then the elusive historian was found, in a corner talking to two men who had been discussing trading pocket knives. He had pulled out his own knife, and a major debate over the merits of each had ensued. No trades followed, however. Later, outside the eating establishment, Clark stopped to discuss deer hunting with a Fish and Wildlife official, then spoke to another person about crops in the area. When Clark left, half of the people there probably felt they knew him, and all seemed to like him. Moreover, he appeared to have the same attitude toward them and had learned things from each person he encountered.

That afternoon Clark dedicated the marker at the Beech Creek Cemetery, attended a reception at the community center, and then headed home to the Bluegrass. That day he had touched various people's lives, had taken history's message to a rural county, and had gained a better understanding of a former governor and his world by walking the same land as had Combs. Clark had continued to be an example of what historians should be and should do. Kentucky would be a much poorer state historically without Tom Clark's books, but it would be an even poorer place, in all respects, without Thomas D. Clark the man.

NOTES

1. John F. Day, *Bloody Ground* (1941; reprint, Lexington: Univ. Press of Kentucky, 1981), 174-75, 179-80, xii, 184.

2. Thomas D. Clark, "Foreword," in Day, *Bloody Ground,* xi-xii.

3. Thomas D. Clark, *The Kentucky* (1942; reprint, Lexington: Henry Clay Press, 1969), 205-11. Material quoted in the text and not otherwise referenced in the notes comes from the author's conversations with Clark over the years.

4. Ibid., 197.

5. Ibid., 214-15.

6. Bill Cunningham, *Kentucky's Clark* (Kuttawa, Ky.: McClanahan Publishing, 1987), 44.

7. Thomas D. Clark, "Local History: A Mainspring for National History," in Richard Jensen et al., *Local History Today* (Indianapolis: Indiana Historical Society, 1979), 29, 41.

8. Cunningham, *Kentucky's Clark,* 114; Rebecca Sharpless, "An Interview with Thomas D. Clark," *OAH Newsletter* 27 (Nov. 1999): 6.

9. Sharpless, "Interview," 6; Cunningham, *Kentucky's Clark,* 43; Clark, "Local History," 34.

10. Quoted in David Osborne and Ted Gaebler, *Reinventing Government* (Reading, Mass.: Addison-Wesley, 1992), 219.

11. Thomas D. Clark, *Footloose in Jacksonian America: Robert W. Scott and His Agrarian World* (Frankfort: Kentucky Historical Society, 1989); John E. Kleber, ed., *The Kentucky Encyclopedia* (Lexington: Univ. Press of Kentucky, 1992); John E. Kleber, ed., *The Encyclopedia of Louisville* (Lexington: Univ. Press of Kentucky, 2001).

12. John Sheffield, *Essay on Poetry,* cited in John Bartlett, *Familiar Quotations,* 15th ed. (Boston: Little, Brown, 1980), 316.

13. Thomas D. Clark, *The Rampaging Frontier: Manners and Humors of Pioneer Days in the South and Middle West* (Indianapolis: Bobbs-Merrill, 1939), 17, 27.

14. Thomas D. Clark, *Pills, Petticoats, and Plows: The Southern Country Store* (Norman: Univ. of Oklahoma Press, 1944), 174; idem, *The Southern Country Editor* (Indianapolis: Bobbs-Merrill, 1948), 294; idem, *The Greening of the South: The Recovery of Land and Forest* (Lexington: Univ. Press of Kentucky, 1984), 24.

15. Thomas D. Clark, "Live Stock Trade between Kentucky and the South," *Register of the Kentucky Historical Society* [hereafter cited as *Register*] 27 (1929): 569-81; idem, "The Ante-bellum Hemp Trade of Kentucky with the Cotton Belt," *Register* 27 (1929): 538-44; idem, "The Slave Trade between Kentucky and the Cotton Kingdom," *Mississippi Valley Historical Review* 21 (1934): 331-42; idem, "Kentucky Education through Two Centuries of Political and Social Change," *Register* 83 (1985): 173-201.

16. Thomas D. Clark, *Agrarian Kentucky* (Lexington: Univ. Press of Kentucky, 1977), x, vii.

17. Thomas D. Clark, *Historic Maps of Kentucky* (Lexington: Univ. Press of Kentucky, 1979).

18. *Lexington Herald-Leader,* July 14, 1998; Lewis Collins and Richard H. Collins, *History of Kentucky,* 2 vols. (1874; reprint, Berea, Ky.: Kentucke Imprints, 1976); William E. Connelley and E. Merton Coulter, *History of*

Kentucky, 5 vols. (Chicago: American Historical Society, 1922). Clark would coauthor his own precollegiate text for schools two years after his *History* appeared. See Thomas D. Clark and Lee Kirkpatrick, *Exploring Kentucky* (New York: American Book Co., 1939). It went through several editions, including ones in 1949 and 1955. Clark also wrote other Kentucky works for a younger audience. See, for example, his *Simon Kenton, Kentucky Scout,* ed. Melba Porter Hay (1943; reprint, Ashland, Ky.: Jesse Stuart Foundation, 1993).

19. Thomas D. Clark, *A History of Kentucky* (New York: Prentice-Hall, 1937), vii. The work has gone through several editions with different publishers and varied fonts and page totals. The 500-some-page 1960 revision, for example, bore the John Bradford Press imprint; the book now in print came out in 1988 as the sixth edition under the auspices of the Jesse Stuart Foundation in Ashland, Ky.

20. Clark, *History* (1960 ed.), 20.

21. Ibid., 240.

22. Ibid., 300.

23. Lowell H. Harrison and James C. Klotter, *A New History of Kentucky* (Lexington: Univ. Press of Kentucky, 1997), [v].

24. Thomas D. Clark, *The Kentucky* (New York: Farrar and Rinehart, 1942); *Lexington Herald-Leader,* July 14, 1998. *The Kentucky* was reprinted in 1969 (Henry Clay Press), with new material added, and again in 1992 (Univ. Press of Kentucky) in a still different version.

25. Clark, *The Kentucky* (1992 ed.), 19.

26. Ibid., 109.

27. Ibid., 409-10, 429.

28. Thomas D. Clark, *Kentucky: Land of Contrast* (New York: Harper & Row, 1968), ix-x.

29. Ibid., 30.

30. Ibid., 91, 199, 147.

31. Ibid., 290.

32. Cunningham, *Kentucky's Clark,* 120.

33. Ibid., 109.

Local Historian

NANCY DISHER BAIRD AND
CAROL CROWE CARRACO

In the late 1970s an administrator at an Ivy League university asserted, "Local and community history may well be one of the fastest growing popular intellectual pursuits in the United States." Historian Thomas D. Clark clearly anticipated this observation fifty years earlier as he pursued graduate studies at the University of Kentucky and at Duke University. His master's thesis was entitled, "The Trade Between Kentucky and the Cotton Kingdom in Livestock, Hemp, and Slaves," and his dissertation dealt with the development of railroads in the South before 1860. Published in 1933 as *The Beginning of the L&N,* it joined an earlier article on the pioneer "Lexington and Ohio Railroad" and was followed by a larger study, *A Pioneer Southern Railroad: From New Orleans to Cairo.*[1]

Clark suggests that the catalyst that precipitated the greatest change in the lives of nineteenth century American towns and villages was the building of railroads (and later the advent of the automobile). Transportation stimulated industry, ended isolation, and changed the tempo of life. For good or bad, transportation changes affected the economics and politics of every community in the nation. Clark's writings on a variety of railroads that connected Kentucky with the Deep South illustrate his point. The Lexington and Ohio, Kentucky's first rail line, was conceived in the late 1820s to aid Lexington's loss of trade center status to river towns and the steamboat. Bluegrass merchants decided that a railroad linking Lexington to Frankfort and the capital to the river port city of Louisville was an economic necessity. Making extensive use of era newspapers, county court records, and legislative acts and journals, Clark related the painful struggle to charter and build this railroad. The tale differs little from those of constructing railroads from Louisville to Nashville, Cairo to New Orleans, and Nashville to Chattanooga, all of which linked the Upper and Lower South.

Those building railroads in the antebellum years, Clark found, encountered numerous difficulties. Towns squabbled over the routes, for example. Wishing to build a line that could carry larger and heavier loads than could be transported by boat, the Louisville and Nashville Company considered two routes. According to Clark, the one through Bowling Green and Russellville was shorter, but a line through Glasgow bypassed Muldraugh's Hill and the Green River, and thus offered fewer engineering obstacles. All communities pledged funds but the people of Bowling Green offered more and won. Residents of Glasgow have never quite forgotten their ancestors' defeat and the resulting commercial cost to that town. The completion of the L&N in 1859 and its Memphis line in 1860 linked the Upper South's three major cities. Small towns along the line also flourished. They constructed warehouses and hotels, opened private schools, attracted new settlers seeking employment and business opportunities, and enjoyed a host of commercial advantages denied to their rail-less neighbors.

Railroads moved more swiftly and carried heavier loads than could riverboats and experienced no problems with sand bars, snags, and other impediments. Unfortunately, they could also move armies and heavy armaments, and during the Civil War these lines became as much a curse to southern residents as they had been a blessing on their completion in prewar days. Although all lines experienced damage, the New Orleans to Cairo perhaps suffered the most severely. Rails had been made into "Jeff Davis Neckties," locomotives were worn out, depots and machine shops had been burned, trade and travel had disappeared, and the company coffers were empty. Nevertheless, within a few years most of the lines were restored and towns again profited from the railroads. In 1877 the New Orleans, Jackson and Great Northern and the Mississippi Central consolidated as the New Orleans, St. Louis and Chicago Company. A few years later the Illinois Central System acquired it. The union by rail of the cotton kingdom and the grain growing belt bound together diverse yet complementary communities.

Another of Clark's early works, *The Rampaging Frontier,* studies the humor of the hearty souls who braved the frontiers of Kentucky, Tennessee, and adjoining states. Using tales unearthed in newspapers, memoirs, travelers' accounts, dusty courthouse records, and other firsthand accounts, Clark weaves anecdotes and commentaries about the everyday affairs that characterized the Old West. His chosen stories about local life—of a duel between "a pair of dunces" in Frankfort, a camp meeting in Rushmore, Ohio, that attracted a drunken band that "cavorted around like Shawnee Indians," a pompous and ignorant Breathitt County justice who issued a "rit" that "cussed" the defendant of "everything that was mean and contrary to the law," a Clay County fellow who bred wolves and claimed bounties for the scalps of their pups—vividly illustrate local life on the rough frontier. Clark relates frontiersmen's tales of snakes the size of giant anacondas, tigers and catamounts that carried off children, and corn-stealing squirrels that raided Kentucky fields before returning to Indiana on shingles they propelled by their tails. The volume includes colorful accounts of brief courtship, festive weddings, philandering husbands, and runaway wives. The frontier was a single woman's paradise, Clark reminds his reader, for men outnumbered them. Although their lives could be hard, frontier gals also enjoyed an unusual degree of independence. Clark tells of a Bourbon County woman who caused her husband to be locked in the county jail while she "took advantage" of his confinement and "disposed of my property and run me in to debt." He also relates tales of the exploitation of women by rascals who loved and left—usually with the women's property. One such person was an itinerant preacher visiting in Louisville. The parson not only made off with his host's wife but, when confronted by the irate husband, proposed to swap a horse for the wife, to which the husband agreed! *The Rampaging Frontier* is filled with local stories that relate the times and conditions of the Old West.[2]

Clark's studies of the country store (*Pills, Petticoats, and Plows*) and country newspaper editors (*The Voice of the Frontier* and *The Southern Country Editor*), likewise use local stories to illustrate regional traditions. Until recent times the country or small-town newspaper has always been the purveyor of news, but few pre-Clark scholars looked closely at these resources as influential in local and eventually regional opinions. In writing his 1948 work about these newssheets, Clark decried the fact that no depository had a representative collection of southern newspapers; microfilm has since answered this void, and research libraries today spend large portions of their budgets in filming and acquiring film of small-town papers.

Editing a country newspaper, Clark argued, was a desirable professional calling in the New South, for it commanded prestige and guaranteed an important position in community affairs. Brief but specific editorials both colored and reflected local feelings, for editors knew the prejudices of their readers, knew what not to print, and knew also that their readers considered them well informed and would therefore value their opinions. An editor was responsible to the readers.

Clark's *Voice of the Frontier* examines early issues of the *Kentucky*

Gazette, in which editor John Bradford exhibited a "vivid thread of emotionalism in reaction to Indian problems" yet expressed little concern for the social and economic problems of the pioneer era. Once the Indian "menace" ended, Bradford's columns contained scant information concerning the proceedings of Congress and the state legislature, but offered more about happenings among the Kentucky settlements and the efforts to make Kentucky a state. A four-page weekly, by the 1790s the newspaper included news items about everything from the executions of Louis XVI and Marie Antoinette and warring in Europe to runaway horses, slaves, and wives (although little about errant husbands). Lists of items for sale (most of which were imported from Philadelphia), court notices, ads about horses standing stud, and other items of local interest filled the columns of the *Kentucky Gazette*. Much of what is known about the early years of Kentucky—and what Kentuckians knew about national and international happenings—comes from the *Kentucky Gazette* and other early papers, including Richmond's *Republican*, Russellville's *Messenger*, Bowling Green's *Spirit of the Times*, and Louisville's *Courier* and *Journal*.[3]

In the post–Civil War years, news and editorials in Louisville's *Courier-Journal* dominated Kentucky's newssheets. From stories about troubles during Reconstruction to editorials damning the Hapsburgs and Hohenzollerns, Henry Watterson and other editors across the South guided public opinion and revealed life in the city as well as the hinterland. But as public opinion reveals in *The Southern Country Editor*, small-town papers nevertheless flourished and reflected local life and sentiments. For example, editors frequently nagged for local improvements. When the editor of the Stanford [Ky.] *Interior Journal* fell through a hole in that town's sidewalk and broke a leg, he lambasted the town fathers for their apathy in caring for the town and making it safe. Of Gov. Luke Blackburn, Kentucky's "father of prison reforms," local papers that previously condemned the sending of "Ku

Kluxers" to prison now criticized Blackburn for pardoning these same "law-breakers and murderers." On the education of women, the McMinnville [Tenn.] *New Era* said that a girl's education "was useful" if she settled down after graduation to "guide the home circle." In the same vein, a Marietta paper indicated "There is no place like home, especially if it is the house of a pretty girl, when they [*sic*] keep a good fire during the cold weather in the parlor and turn the lamps down low to save expenses."[4]

Most papers included bits of humor along with the more serious and enlightening text. Clark quotes a Jackson, Tennessee, paper which reported that a young man on the road to Arkansas overtook an elderly traveler and learned that for the last eighteen years the old gent's goal had been to go to heaven. "Well, if you have been traveling toward heaven for eighteen years," the youngster answered, "and got no nearer to it than Arkansas, you need to take another route."[5]

Like the small-town newspaper, the rapidly vanishing country store, Clark found, is also a local institution that has molded local sentiments and happenings. Clark reports that the few that remain are "exciting museums of antiquated goods and merchandising methods," but that in today's fast-paced society they remain a "placid world of community life. Their stove sides are still forums where domestic affairs and gossip are discussed daily, even where both merchants and their stock have undergone [few] changes." And where else could one purchase, under the same roof, fancy china, perfumed soap, sewing thread, a flower-decked toilet seat, a bag of nails, a horse collar, a hat for church, and a pair of sturdy boots? More than just a one-stop shopping convenience, the country store also served as a center of information and a place where one could leave a message, obtain a small loan, and pay a bill.[6]

Although his biographical sketches are few, with them Clark acquaints readers with not only the individual but the community and the ideals he represented. For example, Clark used Helm Bruce as a means of looking at Louisville's 1905 mayoral election; little of the biography actually concerns this descendant of several early Kentuckians of prominence and his fight to right a political injustice. Nevertheless, in studying the election, Clark placed the "whole socio-political struggle of [post–Civil War] Louisville in perspective . . . [for it] was only a part of the larger and even more sordid American pageant of applying democratic principles and techniques in an age of raw, undisciplined and ever-expanding urban-industrial society." Much of what had made Louisville prosperous, he argues, had also "impoverish[ed] and bankrupt[ed] it morally and politically."[7]

Forty-five election fraud cases came before the Jefferson County Court following the mayoral election in 1905. Helm Bruce served as chief of counsel. In a lengthy, explicit, and well-documented brief, Bruce asserted that the election was so unfair that in essence "there has been no election." The Jefferson County Court disagreed. Bruce then took the cases to the Kentucky Court of Appeals. In his argument before the court, he called for "fair play in Louisville." His appeal was so moving that "not even the rowdy Democratic horde stirred in its seats." The appeals court reversed the lower court's decision by a vote of 4-2, and a few days later the governor appointed Robert Worth Bingham to serve as the new mayor of the Falls City.[8]

Clark concludes his narrative by warning that the court's decision did not end "election thieves and corruptors" but that it was a watershed in both Louisville and Kentucky political history. The Louisville cases, however, revealed "how stupid men could be . . . [that] in the quest for power they trampled basic American institutions underfoot with the blithe excuse that four years of good pickings lay ahead at the courthouse and city hall."[9]

Clark's own concern for preserving Kentucky's state records is well illustrated by his interest in the brief biographies of two amateur historians, Louisvillians Reuben T. Durrett and Rogers Clark Ballard Thruston, who worked to awaken Kentuckians to the need to preserve these local treasures. Durrett, a lawyer and a founder of the Filson Club, became interested in collecting historical materials in his youth. Searching for books relating to the early history of Louisville and the Ohio Valley, he traded when he could, purchased when possible, and amassed a fine collection of rare volumes. He corresponded with numerous historians and literary lights of his day, produced an impressive array of essays, papers, and books, and attracted others who also held an interest in the early history of Kentucky and of Louisville.

In 1884, on the centenary of the publication of John Filson's *The Discovery, Settlement, and Present State of Kentucke,* Durrett gathered a group of history-minded friends at his home, and they formed the Filson Club. (Now the Filson Historical Society). Its mission was to collect and preserve historical manuscripts, books, and other materials related to the old frontier and to prepare and publish papers read at the meetings. Thus began one of the finest research libraries in the Old West and a major publisher of local history. Durrett's home served as the Filson Club's meeting place as well as the club's library. At their monthly gatherings he and other Louisville aristocrats listened to papers written by members of the august group, discussed Kentucky history, sipped crab apple cider, and smoked Filson Club cigars. In his declining years, however, Durrett's own library—and that of the Filson Club—fell into disarray. Materials lay in piles throughout his house and outbuildings. Most of his Filson friends had passed on, no serious scholar announced interest in materials relating to Kentucky or the Ohio Valley, and no library in the state had the means to care for his collection. In fact, no library even cared very well for its own collection! When the state government moved to its new offices in 1908, the nearby Kentucky River "ran full of discarded state records!"[10]

Seeking safety for his life's work, Durrett offered his collection to the state if it would build a fireproof structure in which to house it and the commonwealth's records. He made the same offer to Louisville. But the "small-minded politicians" of the era focused "on grabbing and retaining power and they gave little if any thought to historical preservation." Eventually the books, pamphlets, newspapers, and manuscripts of Durrett's collection went to the University of Chicago. A large collection of Durrett's correspondence is now in The Filson Historical Society, and Tom Clark took four truckloads of materials once stored in Durrett's carriage house and servants' quarters to the Special Collections at the University of Kentucky library.[11]

Clark also took up Durrett's cudgel to preserve state records and for years he sweet-talked, cajoled and harassed members of the legislature on the need to preserve the commonwealth's treasures. In 1958 the State Archives and Records Commission was created and in October, 1982, sixty-nine years after Durrett's death, the dream that he and Tom Clark shared became a reality. The Kentucky Department of Library and Archives moved into its fine modern home, the Clark-Cooper Building, on Coffee Tree Road in Frankfort.

Rogers Clark Ballard Thruston was another local historian about whom Clark wrote. A talented geologist, Thruston spent many years in his youth platting, mapping, photographing, and carefully documenting much of the rugged mountain terrain of Eastern Kentucky for the Geological Survey and the Inter-State Investment Company. The thirteen volumes of notes he kept are a rich source of information for family and area history and have even been used in land cases before the courts. Clark, who has also tramped over mountainsides searching for vague landmarks and boundaries, praised Thruston:

Aside from the prodigious ordeal of surveying up and down steep grades, taking accurate measurements over rocky barriers and cliffs, through heavy forest growth and matted brambles, there was the totally frustrating matter of locating and identifying landmarks which are vague when first established and described. No one who has not tried to locate hacked trees, branches of a creek all bearing the same name, rocks, springs and approximate directions improperly read on a compass and more defectively measured can appreciate the Herculean achievement represented in Thurston's thirteen bound volumes.[12]

In addition to his activities in Appalachian Kentucky, Thruston became an active member of the Filson Club. Among the rather exclusive group of men he "formed a direct human tie" with the rising new generation of "highly competitive and profit motivated Louisville entrepreneurs." Interested particularly in the "human elements of the past," he pursued information, delivered papers before the group, and published a number of articles in the club's quarterly publications. He searched, and hired others to search, court records for facts relating to his family and the signers of the Declaration of Independence. He had photostats made of materials in other state repositories that pertained to Kentucky, including thousands of pieces from the George Rogers Clark papers in the Virginia State Library and the Lyman Draper papers belonging to the State Historical Society of Wisconsin; these copies now belong to the Filson Historical Society. In a letter to a DAR official, he told of visiting Kentucky's archives and finding papers "strewn over the floor . . . being trampled upon." Appalled that public records had been pilfered and grossly mismanaged, he brought to the attention of the state officials the need to preserve state documents, court records, correspondence, newspapers, and other valuable research materials. Eventually he gave his large library, his research materials, and photographs to the Filson Club and on the eve of the Great Depression established an endowment fund for the club of $50,000 and an acquisition fund of $25,000. In his will he bequeathed the club another $125,000. Kentucky's historians owe a great debt to Rogers Clark Ballard Thruston.[13]

And to Tom Clark! Early in his career Clark realized that local history serves as a microcosm of national history, with the added incentive that it is more interesting to people of a particular area. It is the "yeasty and important ingredient in the writing and interpreting of the larger national experience," Clark wrote years later. Clark, like all successful southern writers, tells a good story, but he avoids the pitfalls of family research and/or ancestor worship. "I must make it crystal clear that I am not a genealogist."[14]

For Clark, writing country history is akin to the editing and publishing of a country weekly newspaper; of necessity it must involve a multiplicity of personal names, some of notable and accomplished individuals and some of more humble persons. But, he writes, "my interest and approach has been in the responses; [sic] social, cultural, political and economic that human beings have made to land and place. In Clark County past, these have been deeply personal and forceful."[15]

Clark's history of Clark County and its seat, Winchester, is a somewhat mixed one. No doubt the county and the town have been microcosmic prototypes of all the other Bluegrass counties, but with a discernible difference. There has long existed in Clark County a provincial attachment to a variety of social, cultural, and economic mores. These facts challenge the historian to sort out and be selective on the multiple historic strands that interface through the region's past. The physical nature of the land, environmental impacts, and industrial influences all have contributed heavily to molding the everyday way of life in the county. Throughout the last two centuries there have lingered reminders of close-knit family interrelationships and the sharing of common relationships by blood and community attachment. The fact that several cohesive family and communal groups made the arduous trek from Virginia to the developing western frontier brought about a closeness of families and communities from the county's historic beginnings. The family, immediate and extended, Clark shows, has been a force in shaping the course of history in Clark County.

There exists a contradiction in Clark County's history, however, as is true in all of Kentucky. While the family is revered, its elders have been negligent in providing adequate educational opportunities for rising generations. A partial answer for this deficiency in educational progress, Clark believes, may rest in the fact that settling a virgin country—the construction of housing and outbuildings and the making of a living from stump-laden soil—demanded the expenditure of backbreaking energy rather than intellectual application. The potential for Indian raids and the need for a militia force to free the land from danger likewise were of great concern and absorbed considerable time. None of these efforts demanded learned skills. Added to these tasks were those of opening roads, building milldams, and constructing flatboats and propelling them south loaded with country produce. All of these were labor-intensive undertakings.

Tom Clark shows that social, economic and political changes in Clark County must at all times be viewed from the perspective of the rural-agrarian nature of the provincial society. From the penetration of the wilderness by Euro-American settlers down to the present, agriculture in the broadest sense has been the basis of Clark County's social and economic well-being. Until the latter half of the twentieth century the way of life in Clark County was predominantly land-based, with family farms as the foundation of every aspect of human life. Even in the twenty-first century, while there has been a shifting away from the old method of farming and land management, the importance of the land still exists. In the final analysis, the fundamental changes that have come in the rural-agrarian areas of life have been in the nature and quality of human use of the land.

Much of what Clark discusses in his Bluegrass county history he had formalized ten years earlier in his story of Laurel County. Historical beginnings in Laurel County predate the statutory creation of a separate governing unit. Archeological remains document the fact that early inhabitants wandered through its river valley, tramped out trails and scattered stone artifacts. Later the American Indians hunted its woods and more clearly defined its passageways. With the dawning of Euro-American penetration of the Appalachian Mountains, land scouts, long hunters, and traders tramped across the face of Laurel. Sites in the future Laurel became landmarks for immigrant settlers on their way to central Kentucky. Boone's Trace, blazed in early 1775, became a route of penetration. Later it was superseded by the Wilderness Road, over which a good portion of American pioneers were to travel west. Throughout most of two centuries, Laurel County has been tied to the Wilderness Road and its successor highways. It became the stopping place for immigrants, traders, drovers, travelers, and even opposing armies in the Civil War. With the coming of the railroad in 1882 and the subsequent introduction of the automobile, London, the seat of Laurel County, has been a midway point for the rising domestic and commercial travel into southeastern and eastern Kentucky and between North and South.

Laurel County's population established a long and continuous history of exploiting the land, forest, and mineral resources, creating towns and villages, welcoming an influx of Swiss colonists and missionaries seeking a home for a Methodist college, and establishing the federal court and modern twentieth-century industries. Thus, in microcosm, the history of Laurel County eloquently reflected the broader American experience of pioneering, yeoman farming, and opening an era of extensive commercialization. It has been a prototype of many of the southeastern Kentucky counties.

The historic plight of the Kentucky counties has, since 1780 and the creation of Kentucky County, been the local breeding grounds of politics, of progress or lack of it, and of the shaping of what might be called the Kentucky "turn of mind." County order, will, and deed books constitute a virtual annalistic recording of the social, economic, and political happenings in the county. Spread across their pages are hundreds of names of politicians and humble everyday citizens who filed through courthouse doors to transact business, both trivial and important. The will books in many ways constitute a worldly book of life. The masculine ordainers all but opened the secrets of their hearts, their coffers, and their accumulations of worldly goods. They expressed love and affection for their prospective widows, favored some children, and sent messages of disapproval to others.

The recorded wills and estate inventory records, along with the adjustment of dower rights, are the weaving of the very fabric of life itself in the country. Perhaps the only time many individuals ever appeared in the public records, aside from being called upon to work the roads and pay taxes, was in one of the county record books. Citizens came to the court for a great variety of reasons besides seeing and being seen. They sought adjustments in tax levies, fees for officiating in elections and for guarding prisoners; came to defend themselves against charges of bastardy, thievery, and mayhem; or sought authority for operating ferries, whipping slaves, and inspecting products stored in public warehouses. Political tentacles in some fashion or another reached out from the courthouse to all parts of the county.

The historian learns at the outset that writing about the American experience at the grassroots level involves perpetual mastery of the process of selectivity. Involved is the treatment of personalities, institutions and even human follies. Clark states, "In writing this history [of Clark County] I have been challenged by the fact I had to be selective of the names and the contributions of persons, of local anecdotes and even those commonplace incidents which have given space to the past in rural-agrarian America." A historian might well spend a lifetime "digging nuggets" of information out of official records, private papers, commercial records, and official documents. Laurel and Clark Counties came into existence in an era that literally seethed with the excitement of penetrating virgin land and planting the original foundations of Euro-American civilization in the area. The defense against hostile resistance from competing Indian groups, the austerities of a raw environment, and the heavy demands on human energy were the challenges to human courage and persistence.

In writing about a locality, the historian must always be responsive to the basic forces that are generated in an area and to the elements of personality, the human "lubrication of anecdotes and even with blood relationships unto unnumbered generations when the blood strain grows thin and tattered." In no area of history does the anecdote, factual or devised, assume greater importance than at the grassroots of local human society. Often the anecdote becomes so firmly embedded in local history that it becomes difficult if not downright damaging to separate fact from fiction.[16]

Looking back on the closing years of the twentieth century, it is clear that there has not been a decade in which Clark and Laurel Counties did not undergo change. The first order books of the counties are filled with entries pertaining to the opening of roads and the readjustment of land boundaries, and those of the current era contain entries on the same subjects. The evolution of county roads, turnpikes, railways, and subsequent modern surfaced and numbered federal and state highways clearly reflects social, political, and economic changes.

Tom Clark states that he wrote the two county histories largely because "years ago as head of the Department of History in the University of Kentucky [1942-65] I sought to bring together a group of scholars to produce a searching study of at least five representative counties in Kentucky to determine the grass roots dynamics of the state itself. The effort failed largely because of differing notions as to what might constitute an adequate local history."[17]

The most recent local history book by Clark appeared in the fall of 2002, and it is a valuable addition to the continuing story of the importance of place in the lives of Kentuckians. *The People's House: The Governor's Mansions of Kentucky,* written jointly with Margaret A. Lane, is an informative and amusing account of the occupants of Kentucky's governors' homes. The almost 300-page coffee-table book, with its plethora of photographs, offers glimpses inside the two official residences in which Kentucky's chief executives have resided and often carried on the business of state, for there was no separate governor's office for decades. Yet the tale of Kentucky's governor's "Palace," as it was called for many years, is more than the story of stones, mortar and architectural design; it is an account of the people who lived there and the citizens of the commonwealth who visited. The condensed sociopolitical narrative is replete with humorous stories.

Long ago, Tom Clark declared that local history was a mainspring for national history, for it "performed the sacred mission of giving readers an intimate sense of time and place and of being a part of a community." Certainly, Clark's works have provided a close sense of time and place. Whether writing or speaking about a local light, about a county's past, about the impact of a railroad, the country store or the area newspaper or other entities that shaped local, regional,and national life, Clark has always used, evaluated, and stressed the effect of local on national happenings.[18]

American history "is the account of local communities strung together to form a composite nation," and local historians have traditionally been the authors of these accounts, Clark claims. Speaking to both amateur and professional historians at a workshop about local history, Clark acknowledged the debt of professionally trained historians to a number of fine amateur historians who went before—to Lewis Collins, Henry Howe, and Samuel Hildreth and others who compensated for their lack of access to records with firsthand insight and knowledge. Local history is important, Clark pointed out on another occasion, because "That is where the Bill of Rights resides. That is where the citizen casts his vote and that is where he exercises all other rights. That is where he goes to court, where he sends his prisoners to the penitentiary or to jail, where he sends his patients to hospitals and where he educates his children. There is every reason why local history is important. All those things are important."[19] Because not all Kentuckians are alike, the need for local history is great. Composed of 120 counties, each with its own distinct past, the commonwealth's geographic regions have also divided peoples and encouraged a "localism" in traditions and events that needs to be recorded. Appalachia, until recent years an isolated and sparsely settled area, has been blessed (and cursed) with fine but exploited resources. The Bluegrass, a fertile area and trade center that could compete with any area of the nation, has long been seen—and written about—as "Kentucky," yet it has little in common with other regions. The Pennyroyal and Western Coalfield are highly sectionalized areas, some portions of which are rich in resources, some that had supported subsistence farming, and some that boast productive agricultural land. The Jackson Purchase is an agricultural area, the westernmost portion of which more closely resembles western Tennessee than it does much of Kentucky. The manufacturing and distribution centers of Louisville and Greater Cincinnati are far removed in lifestyle and tradition from the commonwealth's rural areas. Thus each region and each county, distinctly different from the others, has a history that is both different and similar. Collectively they make up the history of Kentucky.

Although local historians in the past seemed to concentrate on pioneer and Civil War topics, Clark has encouraged followers of Clio to look at more recent history and its unlimited number of topics. He has pointed out that American institutions constantly change. What was commonplace yesterday is history today. Recalling just a handful of twentieth-century changes, he urged history-minded students to explore the effects on everyday family and community life of the changeovers from kerosene to electric lights, from the one-room school to huge consolidated systems, from country stores to shopping malls, from church-related charities to tax-supported social services, from cure-all nostrums and home care to modern pharmacies and hospitals. Many of these changes result from progress in transportation and communication. The railroads ended the barriers of isolation or created ghost towns that were bypassed; automobiles and the resulting paved roads and interstates ended all barriers. Many towns in very recent years have struggled with the problem of a dying downtown as businesses have moved toward the interstate, and large areas, once cornfields, have become parking lots. Likewise changes in methods of communication, from the weekly paper and periodic mail delivery to instant TV coverage of world events, have had impact on everyday life. Writing today, Clark could certainly add how the computer and online access to some knowledge have changed youths' attitudes toward libraries!

The plethora of resources available today also encourages the writing of local history. Newspapers, statistical reports, school records, court records, account books, and business records "may lack the glamour and the elements of simplicity of remote pioneering years," Clark has pointed out, but they are nevertheless important. They are also easily accessed. Interviews can also be sources of information, but Clark warns that memories fade and that "just because an individual has, by the grace of God, reached a ripe old age is no assurance he is an historical oracle." Oral histories should be used to supplement official records, not replace them. "Much of the chatter now being cap-

tured on magnetic tape in the name of oral history is no more significant than the cries of predatory starlings," Clark warned in his colorful way with words.[20]

Clark has other words of wisdom for writers of local history, and
they are good advice for everyone. A historian should do more than
chronicle a litany of events; good history contains perspective and interpretation. History should never be dull or unimaginative. A master storyteller himself who, someone once said, could "turn a lectern
into a cracker barrel," Clark emphasizes that style and grace are important. One has only to read a few tales from *The Rampaging Frontier, The Southern Country Editor, The People's House,* or other works
by Clark to learn how effective the narrative can become when good
stories and clever twists of words punctuate it. He also warns that a
manuscript should always be read by an outside critic before it is submitted for publication. Even the most "mature historian" cannot "prepare a manuscript of acceptable quality without the aid of an objective and critical editorial reader," he warns. Clark also notes that authors should be able to accept criticism—something that everyone
finds difficult—on a labor of love. "It takes a stout heart to accept
criticism which suggests material revisions of a manuscript or more
research and a different organization," he warns. On the other hand,
it is far better to eliminate mistakes, correct awkward sentences, re-
think erroneous conclusions and improve inadequate research before
it appears in print.[21]

In all his activities, Clark has been the historian's best friend. Clark
believes that the current generation of historians stands in a golden
field of commonplace subjects that should be explored. Perhaps one
of his greatest contributions has been to encourage students and others passionately interested in the past to explore and write about their
own locale. Whether a member of a local historical society, a student,
a fledgling historian, or a seasoned scholar, Clark's encouragement and

influence have been and will continue to be felt for years to come. For decades he has traversed the state, speaking to local historical groups and student organizations. Those who have heard him speak about Kentucky have been moved by his knowledge and ardor for history; those who have listened to his passionate plea for the collection and preservation of materials have surely found it difficult to destroy a single scrap of paper; and those who have read his books and journal and newspaper articles are richer for the experience.

NOTES

1. David A. Gerber, "Local and Community History: Some Cautionary Remarks on an Idea Whose Time Has Returned," *History Teacher* 13 (Nov. 1979): 7.

2. Thomas D. Clark, *The Rampaging Frontier: Manners and Humors of Pioneer Days in the South and Middle West* (Indianapolis: Bobbs-Merrill, 1939), 152, 167, 287.

3. Thomas D. Clark, ed., *The Voice of the Frontier: John Bradford's Notes on Kentucky* (Lexington: Univ. Press of Kentucky), xi.

4. Thomas D. Clark, *The Southern Country Editor* (Indianapolis: Bobbs-Merrill, 1948), 100, 121.

5. Ibid., 126.

6. Thomas D. Clark, *Pills, Petticoats, and Plows: The Southern Country Store* (Indianapolis: Bobbs-Merrill, 1944), 11.

7. Thomas D. Clark, *Helm Bruce, Public Defender: Breaking Louisville's Gothic Political Ring, 1905* (Louisville: Filson Club, 1973), vi, 3.

8. Ibid., 47, 49.

9. Ibid., 51, 55.

10. Thomas D. Clark, "Reuben T. Durrett and His Kentuckiana Interests and Collection," *Filson Club History Quarterly* 56 (Oct. 1982): 356.

11. Ibid., 354-55.

12. Thomas D. Clark, "Rogers Clark Ballard Thruston: Engineer, Isolationist and Benevolent Kentuckian," *Filson Club History Quarterly* 58 (Oct. 1984): 416.

13. Ibid., 423, 430.

14. Thomas D. Clark, *Clark County, Kentucky: A History* (Clark County Historical Society, 1995), 362, xiii.

15. Ibid., 361-62.

16. Ibid., xviii.

17. Ibid., 362.

18. Thomas D. Clark, "Local History: A Mainspring for National History," in *Local History Today: Papers Presented at Four Regional Workshops for Local Historical Organizations in Indiana, June 1978-April 1979* (Indianapolis Historical Society, 1979), 51.

19. Ibid., 29; Bill Cunningham, *Kentucky's Clark* (Kuttawa, Ky.: McClanahan Publishing, 1987), 114.

20. Clark, "Local History," 45.

21. Ibid., 35.

Southern Historian

CHARLES P. ROLAND

By any gauge Professor Thomas D. Clark is one of the nation's most renowned living historians, the honored patriarch of the discipline. He is a remarkably productive scholar, the author of thirty-two books. He is also an extraordinarily versatile scholar, having written authoritatively in many fields of American history, including that of the American South.

One is tempted to say that he imbibed southern history with his mother's milk. He is southern to the marrow of his bones, with a regional quality that shows spectacularly in his speech and mannerisms and in virtually every line of his writing. I met Professor Clark in the spring of 1947 during my first semester of graduate school at Louisiana State University. He came there to deliver the Walter Lynwood Fleming Lectures in Southern History, a distinguished annual series of addresses sponsored by the university's history department. His topic was "The Rural Press and the New South."

When I first learned the title of his program, the subject seemed to me too ordinary to serve the purpose of a scholarly series, and excruciatingly dull. I had grown up in an area sprinkled with country newspapers, one of them in my hometown. I had read their parochial editorials, their humdrum write-ups on daily events, and their overblown descriptions of local social affairs. But Clark made the subject come alive, and I quickly warmed to his down-home style and unaffected bearing.

Unquestionably I was attracted to him because we shared a common culture. He was a native of Mississippi and I of West Tennessee, which is often said to be a northward extension of Mississippi. Our speech was markedly similar and we were attuned to identical religious, social, and economic outlooks. He often hails me as being a product of the canebrakes of West Tennessee, a breed of which he is no doubt a connoisseur. We both grew up in an area and an era of cotton agriculture, and both picked cotton in our youth. We grew up surrounded by a multitude of African Americans who were called colored people by the "better" whites of the area. Though both of our families followed the prevailing practice of institutional and social racial segregation, they believed that treating blacks with kindness was a compelling religious mandate as well as an inalienable social obligation.

To have disliked Tom Clark would have been virtually impossible. His pungent speech and unfeigned friendliness tended to create an instant bond with us students and all others who attended the lectures and receptions conducted in his honor by the Louisiana State University history department. He did not talk down to students but instead as if they were his peers. This bond was established the more quickly and firmly as a result of the relationship he held with the chairman of the history department, Professor Bell I. Wiley, who was also my major professor and whom I was serving as a graduate research assistant. The two had been fellow graduate students in working on their master's degrees at the University of Kentucky some twenty years before.

One could not be an active member of the history profession in the years of my apprenticeship without hearing stories about Tom Clark, who was by then a legendary figure as a scholar, a teacher, and a department chairman. I took in all of the stories. Then in the fall of 1955 I again had an opportunity to make close contact with him when I delivered a talk to the Kentucky Civil War Roundtable in Lexington, Kentucky. He was a charter member of the organization and a prominent figure among those who ran it. They entertained me sumptuously at the homes of various members. I particularly recall a post-dinner party at the residence of Squire Winston Coleman, who was both a successful businessman and a serious amateur historian. We lifted glasses and shared Civil War lore while the firelight danced on the blade of Confederate General John Hunt Morgan's sword in its frame above the mantel.

By the time I came to the University of Kentucky department of history in 1970, Professor Clark was no longer there; in 1966 he had accepted the position of Sesquicentennial Professor of History at Indiana University. That is, he was no longer at the University of Kentucky in the flesh. But his intellectual and academic presence remained there in the form of the history department he had built in his years as chairman, and in the Special Collections department at the University library and the University Press of Kentucky, in the founding of both of which he had been the moving spirit.

He retired from Indiana University in 1973, and he and his wife returned to Lexington to live. During the years he was at Indiana University I had little personal contact with him, but since his move back to Lexington we have become warm friends. This relationship has given me an opportunity to become acquainted with Tom Clark the man as well as Tom Clark the scholar and icon.

My most pleasurable contacts with him have been informal—chats at the social occasions of the Kentucky Civil War Roundtable or at lunches together at the University of Kentucky faculty club or in home visits with the Clarks. The similarity of our social and cultural backgrounds has greatly facilitated these conversations. So also has the coincidence of our having been fellow southern historians over a period of several decades, though he preceded me by some twenty years. We sometimes talk about many of our colleagues of the past whom we have known and enjoyed, such as Professor Clement Eaton or Professor Holman Hamilton of the University of Kentucky, Professor E. Merton Coulter or Professor Joseph Parks of the University of Georgia, Professor Frank Owsley or Professor William C. Binkley of Vanderbilt University, or Professor Wendell Holmes Stephenson of Tulane University. One of Clark's more interesting accounts is that of accompanying Professor John Crowe Ransom, a distinguished professor of English at Vanderbilt University and Kenyon College, to put in the mail the manuscript of the celebrated southern agrarian manifesto *I'll Take My Stand.*

Tom Clark's early years in rural Mississippi gave him a colorful rural vocabulary that he frequently employs metaphorically to describe human behavior. He once said of a woman who had approached him in an obvious state of perturbation, "I could see she had her tail over the spatter board." I understood precisely what he meant because I could remember when as a child visiting my rural grandparents I had witnessed the agitation of a horse that had caught its tail over the spatter board of the buggy it was pulling. Clark also once said of a colleague who had been involved in a campus movement Clark disapproved of, "I caught so-and-so with wool between his teeth." No explanation was required for anyone reared in the canebrakes of West Tennessee.

He produced his master's thesis on the topic "Trade between Kentucky and the Cotton Kingdom in Livestock, Hemp, and Slaves," and he wrote his doctoral dissertation at Duke University on the role of the railroads in the economy of the South prior to the Civil War. His first book was an outgrowth of these interests. He was now an instructor in history at the University of Kentucky. Published in 1933, the volume was titled *The Beginning of the L&N: The Development of the Louisville and Nashville Railroad and Its Memphis Branches from 1836 to 1860.* "What the railroad has done for the United States as a whole," he said, "the Louisville and Nashville Railroad has done for the South."[1] He generalized that as an essential link between the South and the Northwest, and combined with the Nashville and Chattanooga Railroad, the L&N was "on the verge of revolutionizing the economic system of the South in 1860."[2]

Three years after the appearance of his book on the L&N, Clark brought out another railroad study titled *A Pioneer Southern Railroad from New Orleans to Cairo.* It rendered an account of the manner in which the Illinois Central Railroad acquired the various local railroads in western Tennessee and Mississippi and combined them to form a unified system that ran parallel to the Mississippi River and linked New Orleans with the northern line of the Illinois Central at Cairo, Illinois. This enabled the Louisiana port city to reach the grain and livestock supply of the Northwest without having to rely on the slow-moving boats that plied the river.

The years following the publication of his volume on the L&N were devoted to research on what was to become a seminal work in southern history, an intensive study of one of the region's distinctive institutions during the decades after the Civil War, the country store. His book *Pills, Petticoats, and Plows: The Southern Country Store* was published in 1944. It showed how the country store grew out of the changed social and economic patterns in the South during the years of Reconstruction. These "cross-roads emporiums of cheap merchandise," to borrow his colorful terminology, sprang up at innumerable rural road intersections and villages and often formed the nuclei of new communities.[3]

The stores were, he wrote, symbols of the creation of a new economic system out of the wreckage of the old. "Perhaps no other southern institution more nearly embodied so much of the intimate story of the New South."[4] And again, "They quickly became the heartbeat and pulse of a good portion of American business. In their own communities they were centers of every sort of neighborhood activity. Everything of importance that ever happened either occurred at the store or was reported there immediately."[5]

The store was an essential economic institution in a predominantly rural area. It provided to its country clients the goods, wares, and many of the services that were available to city folk in the aggregation of grocery stores and meat markets, hardware stores, department stores, pharmacies, banks, even physicians' offices. To its customers the country general store represented a combination of all the above.

To begin with, the store stocked an immense assortment of items, from corsets to coffins, from crop seed and guano fertilizer to plows and cultivators, from salt pork to hoop cheese to oysters, from purgatives to paregoric and Lydia Pinkham's compound for female complaints, from brogans to women's lingerie and men's work jeans and denim overalls and jumpers, from frog gigs and fishhooks to shotguns and pistols. Clark offers earthy and sometimes exuberant comments on many of these products: how, for example, the corsets were designed to accommodate the slenderest of waists but the most heroic of busts and hips. Hidden in secret drawers and dispensed with a furtive look and a deft sleight of hand were the contraceptives of the times. Whatever necessities or rustic luxuries a customer might require, the store endeavored to supply.

An essential function of the store that ran parallel to the function of supply was that of credit. As a rule the customers, white or black, were without cash. The only way they could purchase, and therefore the only way the store could sell, was through a crude system of credit, the much-denounced crop-lien system. The merchant extended credit to his customer, placing the transaction "on account" in his ledger, and took as surety a lien on the customer's coming crop of cotton.

The account was balanced when the crop was harvested. The store ledgers recorded purchases for as little as a nickel's worth of candy, or for such mundane but vitalizing activities as the procreative services of the merchant's bull.

The store was also the local communications center, the medium through which rural southerners gained touch with the world. The newly invented telephone assisted this service greatly because the store, along with the doctor, usually installed the first instrument in the locality. Through this connection the merchant often found himself drawn into the role of intermediary and guarantor for his clients. As Clark put it, "When a man asked a merchant to call a doctor for him, the doctor nearly always attempted to secure the merchant's endorsement of the visit; and in this way many a sleepy storekeeper faced by an anxious father with a grassy cotton crop and a sick child agreed to stand good for a bill which in other and less appealing circumstances he would have refused."[6]

The store was the gathering place of the men of the area, the place for conversation and debate. Around the stove in cold weather, or on the front porch in hot weather, every conceivable topic of interest was thrashed out in talk. These were the scenes of "gabbling, whittling, yarn spinning, chewing, dipping and sly nipping at the bottle."[7] The merchants protected their stores against the barrage of tobacco juice by placing sandboxes at strategic places about the premises, especially around the stoves.

The role of the store as a gathering and talking place gave it immense political influence. In the southern struggle to overthrow the radical Republican state governments during Reconstruction, and to reassert white supremacy, the store was frequently the organizing locale for the militant South Carolina Red Shirts and other groups of like mission throughout the region. The drummers, or traveling salesmen, who supplied the stores became important agents of communication and opinion. The flamboyant Louisiana political tycoon Huey P. Long gained much of his political appeal while serving in his early years as a salesman for a patented shortening by the name of Cottalene. His acquaintance with innumerable country store proprietors in Louisiana gave him an invaluable cadre of supporters when he turned his talents to politics.

Clark saw the country stores as an organic part of the society in which they existed. Though he admitted that some proprietors were grasping Shylocks who cheated their illiterate or semi-literate customers, or who charged exorbitant interest on their accounts, he asserted that the preponderance of evidence shows that proprietors were simply an element in an inefficient furnishing system rather than being the system itself. He said also that as an agency of credit the stores played an indispensable role in the new agricultural South's scramble to get on its feet. They were, he concluded, as vital an institution to the society of the South as were two more celebrated institutions of the region: the church and the Democratic Party. *Pills, Petticoats, and Plows* is recognized as a classic work in the economic, social, and political history of the postwar South.

In 1948 Clark brought out a volume bearing the title *The Southern Country Editor*, a study of another of the most influential figures of the rural South. In Clark's judgment, the country newspapers filled a genuine need in the years immediately after the Civil War by providing a sense of direction to society and a hopefulness that enabled the people to endure the vicissitudes of Reconstruction. The newspapers enhanced the lives of the common folk by publishing the birth, marriage, and death of every citizen and by recording the histories of their various communities. They welcomed newcomers into their neighborhoods; they editorialized on the need for improved farming methods and the introduction of industry.

The rural editors offered their readers advice on virtually every field of human endeavor, including such personal areas as health, marriage, childrearing, and proper conduct and attire in church. "Ladies should take off their hats in church," wrote one journalist. "No preacher can inspire a man who is looking into a lob-sided aggregation of dead birds, stuffed weasels, chameleon skins, ribbons, beads, jets, sticks, straw flowers, corn tassels, and thistledown. It makes a sinner feel lost in the wilderness."[8]

Political discussions were heated and strongly slanted against the Republican party. As long as the editors remained within the Democratic party they could disagree on various other issues. Professor Clark said the rural editors "served as persistent guardians of Southern political traditions," and he credited them with being largely responsible for the relative political solidarity of the South.[9]

The most perplexing subject addressed by the country editors was the most perplexing of all southern situations: race relations. The editors in general shared the views of their readers on this point: they believed that blacks were by nature lazy. Many editors believed much worse: that blacks were wild animals or, worse still, that they were sensual fiends. The editors staunchly supported the segregation of the races. Though a majority of them probably disapproved of lynching in theory, they published horror stories of the rapes of white women by black men, and they often defended the lynching of blacks accused of such outrages. Twentieth-century editors toned down such writings, and a handful of journalists toward the middle of the century exhibited liberal sentiments toward blacks. Clark admitted that many editors continued to hold the older views, yet he concluded optimistically, "But they are dwindling and the liberals are in the ascendant."[10]

Also in 1948 the published version of Clark's Fleming Lectures, *The Rural Press and the New South*, appeared in print. It represented a succinct supplement to the larger work on the country editor.

In 1961 Clark produced another truly groundbreaking work on

the region, *The Emerging South*. This time he was writing about his own era, roughly 1920 to 1960, and thus was able to enhance his research into the records with his personal experiences and observations. He did so with his characteristic shrewd insights and colorful expressions. His book was a pioneer comprehensive study of the South during the period under consideration.

He began his narrative with a description of having recently made a bittersweet and memory-laden drive down a Mississippi road that he had traversed countless times in his youth. It was a road once pitted with mud holes and interspersed with rickety bridges, each of which had to be "negotiated according to its own form of treachery."[11] He told of having hauled thousands of feet of pine lumber and crossties and innumerable loads of cotton along this road. He recalled the spreading cotton fields that lay along its course, and the cabins once occupied by large families of black folk who tilled the soil laboriously with mule-drawn plows and hand tools. The entire area lived under the shadow of crisis.

But the author of this book looked at a vastly different South from the one in which he had grown up. He saw a South in marked transition. Beginning with a discussion of the earlier physical conditions of southern people, focusing on the ravages of hookworm and malaria, he traced the virtual demise of these enervating maladies, but acknowledged the continuing dire presence of tuberculosis. He also traced developments in knowledge of the genetics of the cotton plant, the emergence of the mechanical cotton picker, and the steady shift of cotton production from the old Confederate states to West Texas and the American Southwest. He concluded with an apt figure of speech: "The ancient marriage bond between the old cotton-growing South and King Cotton has been renegotiated as a common law agreement by which each can make promiscuous adventures without seriously compromising the other."[12]

Clark showed that as cotton lost its preeminence in southern agriculture, grains, grazing, tree farming, and poultry production made immense gains. These changes sharply altered and improved the appearance of the southern landscape, overcoming to a significant degree the earlier ravages of soil erosion. "Today," he said, "a sea of green obliterates the ancient corrugation of cotton rows and is a vital factor in the regional economy. . . . The traditional red splotches that once ran from farm to farm in leprous patterns are disappearing."[13]

Clark showed also that the growth of southern industry has equaled the remarkable changes in southern agriculture. This has come about through the exploitation of regional natural resources, the abundance of unorganized labor, and the active participation of state governments in developing programs designed to "Balance agriculture with Industry." These plans have allowed counties and municipalities to offer inducements to industries in the form of building and tax concessions. In his words, this represented a victory for Henry W. Grady, the dynamic and eloquent Atlanta newspaper editor who had long urged his region to industrialize itself. The vast changes in agriculture and industry brought vast demographic changes as well. At the beginning of the era covered by this study the overwhelming majority of southerners resided and made their living on farms. At the close of the era this was true of less than half of the southern population.

Clark said that education has always been the South's greatest challenge. All southern schools suffered from a shortage of money; schools for blacks, which were separate from the white schools at all levels, suffered far more severely. Beginning in the 1940s the region made strenuous efforts to catch up with the rest of the nation in educational quality, but the practice of racial segregation held fast. Only the intervention of the Federal government, particularly the Supreme Court's decision in *Brown* v. *the Board of Education*, brought an end to legal separation of the races in the schools. Clark was optimistic that this change would eventually work smoothly. He believed that only a few blacks would desire to enter the white schools, and that the urbanization of the population would ultimately solve the immemorial southern racial problem.

He ended his book on a cautious note of hope for increasing prosperity and happiness in the region. The South speaks with two voices, he said. One voice looks to a brightening future; the other to a dark past. He believed the evidence pointed to a brightening future.

In 1984 Clark published *The Greening of the South: The Recovery of Land and Forest.* This work dealt with a subject that moved him deeply in the historical, regional, and personal sense, and, at a higher level, in the philosophical sense. He accused historians of having been cotton-blinded, concentrating on staple agriculture, slavery, sectional politics, and "wasted" southern society, to the neglect of another story just as dramatic and important: the story of the southern forests.

He gave in this volume an account of the ruthless exploitation of the South's great natural forests, and how this trend has been reversed, at least to a heartening extent. He opened the book on a note that sounds through all of his writings on the South, a note sometimes dominant, sometimes subdued, a note of nostalgia. "As a boy growing up in the pine-hardwood forests of central Mississippi about the headwaters of the Pearl River, I was privileged to see the great monarchs that had stood for centuries."[14] Sadly, he was destined also to see the destruction of most of the last stands of these ancient trees.

He employed tropes drawn from southern history in his account of the cutting of the regional forests without regard to the future. The northern lumber companies that perpetrated the deed were "carpetbaggers." Southern lumber companies that participated in the act did so not only out of greed but also because of a folk attitude that looked upon forests as being a barrier to the advance of civilization. To him, they were the "scalawags" of the lumber industry. The lumbermen were joined in attacking the trees by the extractors of turpentine and tar from the southern pines. The assault on the forests reached a frenzy during the years of World War I. In 1914 the lumbermen harvested 2,549 billion board feet of timber from the states of West Virginia, Kentucky, and Tennessee, over 70 percent of the amount cut since 1880 in that area.

Clark turned with obvious pleasure to the story of scientific forestry and the restoration of woods to much of the South. It is a story of a happy linking of governmental policy and private enterprise. United State Secretary of the Interior Carl Schurz, who was acquainted with the forestry practices of his native Germany, and Gifford Pinchot, the enlightened head of the Forestry Division of the Department, played important roles, as did George W. Vanderbilt and the scientifically trained forester Carl Alwin Schenck, whom Vanderbilt placed in charge of his 100,000-acre Biltmore tract in North Carolina. With Vanderbilt's support in 1898, Schenck opened the Biltmore Forestry School near Asheville, North Carolina, which trained young men from throughout the South in scientific forestry. Schenck took his students to Germany for strenuous practical work in the forests there. The trained foresters carried back to their own states the doctrines and methods learned at the Biltmore School and in the German forests. These methods included selective cutting of mature trees for marketing and the condemning of the ancient practice of burning the forests for the purpose of clearing the land for pasture and for flushing out game. A rising national public concern resulted in 1911 in the passage by Congress of the Weeks law authorizing that body to purchase land to be set aside as national forests. The groundwork was laid for the revival of the forests of the South, causing Clark to write in a historian's retrospective his anticipation of things to come: "Caught up in the economic depressions of the early

1920s and the Great Depression of the 1930s, the South had one ray of economic hope. The era of its second forest was dawning."[15]

Clark described the inception of that second forest, with emphasis on the creation and work of the Southern Forest Experiment Station, a federal installation with its main base in New Orleans and substations elsewhere in the region. During the Great Depression the federal Civilian Conservation Corps planted more than a billion trees on cutover southern land. A few years later the federally run Tennessee Valley Authority established tree-seedling nurseries and provided the seedlings without cost to landowners who would plant them in marginal lands. The efforts of the TVA nurseries were supplemented by the work of state and corporate nurseries. By 1973, 1.3 million acres had been reforested from these sources.

Inducing the South to turn to tree culture by providing a market for its products was the discovery of methods of using the pulp of southern pines to make newsprint and other papers. Many individuals participated in this development, but its hero was the Savannah chemist Charles H. Herty, who found a chemical bleaching formula for neutralizing the resin content of the pine pulp. Eventually the use of this pulp for making paper led to what Clark, on a triumphal note, called "The Grand March South" of the American paper industry.[16]

In using the term "The Greening of the South," Clark had in mind chiefly the return of the South to forest. He indicated a deep love of the South and a profound interest in its future as well as its history. He welcomed the twin developments of reforestation and the non-lumber industries as a means of salvation for southerners. To him, this was much more than an academic subject. In addition to being a quintessential southerner, he is involved personally in the greening of the region. He owns sizeable tracts of timberlands in Kentucky, South Carolina, and his native Mississippi. On this topic, and all others involving the South, he spoke from the heart as well as the head.

Clark has made many notable contributions to southern history in addition to his major monographs on various subjects within the field. In 1956 he edited and published a two-volume work titled *Travels in the Old South: A Bibliography*, and six years later a companion set of two volumes titled *Travels in the New South: A Bibliography*. Together these contained 1705 entries: summarized and evaluated accounts of travelers through the South. These books represented a stupendous accomplishment and a boon of like importance to everyone interested in the history of the region.

In 1959 Clark published a book that was both historical and advisory titled *Three Paths to the Modern South: Education, Agriculture, and Conservation*. In 1967 he and his University of Kentucky history department colleague Professor Albert D. Kirwan collaborated in the production of a general history of the post–Civil War South titled *The South Since Appomattox: A Century of Regional Change*. Six years later Clark produced an anthology of writings on the New South titled *The South Since Reconstruction*.

He has also made significant contributions other than his research and writing. He has taught southern history to countless students, and has directed some fifteen to twenty doctoral students in the field. As chairman of the University of Kentucky history department from 1942 to 1966 he developed within it what many have said was the nation's foremost center for the study of southern history. He has served as the president of the Southern Historical Association (and of the Mississippi Valley Historical Association, known today as the Organization of American Historians) and as managing editor of the *Journal of Southern History* from 1948 to 1952; and he has played a major role in the collection and preservation of the primary sources for research in southern history.

We salute Thomas D. Clark as the dean of southern historians.

NOTES

1. Thomas D. Clark, *The Beginning of the L&N: The Development of the Louisville and Nashville Railroad and Its Memphis Branches from 1836 to 1860* (Louisville: Standard Printing, 1933), 7.

2. Ibid., 53.

3. Thomas D. Clark, *Pills, Petticoats, and Plows: The Southern Country Store* (Indianapolis: Bobbs-Merrill, 1944), 22.

4. Ibid.

5. Ibid., 32.

6. Ibid., 101.

7. Ibid., 47.

8. Thomas D. Clark, *The Southern Country Editor* (Indianapolis: Bobbs-Merrill, 1948), 43.

9. Ibid., 303.

10. Ibid., 209.

11. Thomas D. Clark, *The Emerging South* (New York: Oxford Univ. Press, 1961), 3.

12. Ibid., 56.

13. Ibid., 72-73.

14. Thomas D. Clark, *The Greening of the South: The Recovery of Land and Forest* (Lexington: Univ. Press of Kentucky, 1984), xi.

15. Ibid., 53.

16. Ibid., 114.

Part III. The Advocate

Agrarian

William E. Ellis

Since his arrival in the commonwealth, Thomas Dionysius Clark has exhorted his fellow Kentuckians to learn from history and from our past mistakes. Praised by journalist John Ed Pearce as "The Sage of Kentucky" and described by Pearce's fellow journalist Al Smith as "progressive, optimistic, extremely energetic, and in so many ways the good citizen," Tom Clark has an uncanny grasp of almost every facet of our heritage. Unfortunately, his gentle admonitions have often fallen on deaf ears. He understands, better than anyone else, the role of agriculture in America's history and in that of his adopted state.

Well into his ninety-ninth year, during an interview in late 2002,[1] Clark described his origins and upbringing as part of the agrarian South. "I was born when cotton was in full bloom, the middle of July," he affirmed. "I grew up with a cotton boll in my hand." Raised on a subsistence family farm, he knew the pleasures as well as the pain of a rural lifestyle. He had to work hard and forego many of the advantages of city life as a boy.

Clark came from sturdy yeoman stock. His mother was an elementary school teacher who instilled in her son the rudiments of an education that spurred him on to greater search for knowledge and meaning in an increasingly complex world.

As for life on the farm, he enjoyed the thrill of being "an emotional, spiritual part of the land, with it seeping up between your toes." He loved the wildlife and the woods. "It had a real attraction," he maintained. "I never lost it."

But there were portents of the future that an intelligent farm boy could not mistake in early twentieth-century Mississippi. "In 1911— I can remember this as vivid as if it were twenty minutes ago," he recalled, "the local paper kept saying this scourge was coming: the boll weevil. I was eight years old. I went up just to the edge of the cotton field and looked in a white bloom and there was that little bug. I couldn't have been looking at my fate more clearly than when I saw that little bug in that white bloom."

The Clarks remained on the farm, but times were changing. An unexpected incident altered the youth's life, further tugging him away from a life on the farm. "I heard a bell ring at an aunt's funeral," he remembered, and finding its origin on a dredge boat helped change his world. At the age of sixteen he went to work clearing the Tallahega Swamp at the head of the Pearl River. Though he began as a cabin boy, he soon found himself in the arduous work of transforming the swamp into a waterway.

The miseries and hazards of such work included "mud, snakes, mosquitoes, and malaria." After two years of such toilsome labor he did not return to the family farm, but attended an agricultural high school, running the school's farm in the summertime. Graduating in 1925, he pondered what to do with his life. When asked if he thought at that time of returning to a lifetime of farming, he replied: "No, I definitely did not want to stay in agriculture, because it was fading by that time."

But, it was not easy for a young man with limited resources to escape a southern subsistence farm. To attend the University of Mississippi he had to raise yet another cotton crop, one that miraculously avoided the dreaded boll weevil because it was semi-isolated in the woods. There followed graduate education at the University of Kentucky and at Duke and the first teaching jobs in what would become a long and illustrious career. About teaching Clark avowed: "I can truthfully say, without any reservation, that I thoroughly enjoyed it."

If Clark's attachment to the soil physically lessened with the beginning of a university career, it was no less spiritually and philosophically intense. Developing into one of the nation's premier historians, he "never lost interest in the land." His research and writing have most often expressed a perceptive rurality. In his books, articles, and essays, from local history to that of the nation, I think he is most comfortable, and most eloquent, when writing about agriculture because he understands it so well. A firm believer in "geographical determinism," he recognizes the limitations imposed by frontier conditions, as well as the heartaches of pioneering. Many pioneers'had "a dream of an Eden that never developed." To Clark the westward movement has been overly sentimentalized. "History is a wicked thing," he said. "You'd think Daniel Boone single-handedly created the American frontier. That's the romantic way. It was hard, hard, hard. Can you imagine getting up in the middle of the night with a child that is sick, terribly sick. By noon the next day on the trail, it's dead. And you have to go and dig a grave and bury it and drive on."

Clark has a firm grasp of the agrarian world. In his histories of the frontier including *The Great American Frontier, Frontier America, Footloose in Jacksonian America: Robert W. Scott and His Agrarian World,* and *The Rampaging Frontier,* he showed his depth of knowledge of the agrarian past. In his felicitous style, he summed up one of the state's enduring problems in *Agrarian Kentucky*: "If the rural Kentuckian during the past two centuries had invested his material resources as recklessly as he supported his public schools," Tom scolded, "he would have been more thoroughly bankrupted than the biblical prodigal son" (vii). Crusading for improved education has always been one of his major thrusts.

Other books, such as *The Emerging South, Three American Frontiers, The South Since Appomattox,* and *Kentucky: Land of Contrast,* reveal Clark's ability to discern the change, often quite fitful, that has been endemic as agriculture has given way to industrialization and modernization.

In *Three Paths to the Modern South: Education, Agriculture, and Conservation,* lectures published for Mercer University's prestigious Lamar Memorial Series, this tough-minded critic found an answer to the region's woes. "Nostalgic and romantic southerners were often captivated by promise of the agrarian way of life. . . . To the realist it was clear that it was bogged down in debt, poor health, low personal efficiency, illiteracy, and deep personal frustration" (xi). The answer, of course, was and is: education, education, education.

I have always thought that some of Clark's greatest insights have been about social history. His keen eye has let us see into the roles of the rural press and rural entrepreneurs in *The Southern Country Editor, The Rural Press and the New South,* and *Pills, Petticoats, and Plows: The Southern Country Store* as exemplars of that way of life. His stress has always been on the practical, work-a-day world of the poorer and middling classes. He has not had as much to say about the genteel plantation South, preferring instead the yeoman farmer and his struggles.

It is this realism that has marked Clark's view of American agriculture. As a youth he witnessed the last days of the "rape the land and get out" mentality practiced by the big Mississippi timber companies. In *The Greening of the South: The Recovery of Land and Forest* he told the story of the pillaging of southern forests into the early 1920s and the beginning of recovery in the New Deal. The profligacy of the earlier time included wasting millions of board feet of lumber in building unused wooden transport ships during World War I.

Much the same thing happened in the commonwealth. In *The*

Kentucky, his history of the Kentucky River in the Rivers of America series, he interviewed the last of the old rivermen who, unknowingly, wasted much of the Kentucky forests. Demonstrating his forte in cultural and social history, Clark told how the Kentucky River remained the center of the commonwealth's life for so long.

Clark never just wrote about the agricultural past, he became active in the rejuvenation of the land. He put in practice the best type of agrarianism, a realism based just as much on his concern for the future as for the past. Well into his nineties he raised a substantial vegetable garden each year, which kept him in touch with the ebb and flow of the seasons and the capriciousness of weather. Although he had long ago left the weevil-ravaged fields of his youth, he was grounded in agricultural reality.

It is this practicality, an agricultural pragmatism, that leads me to call Clark an agrarian realist. Using scientific knowledge, he has sensed what is best for the land and its management for the future. With soil played out from overuse, he has overseen developing models of silviculture, the art of cultivating a forest, in three states. On the old Clark family farm in Mississippi, at Turnbull Plantation (the ancestral home of his first wife, Elizabeth Turner Clark) in South Carolina, and in Kentucky, he dedicated debilitated land to raising trees. In Mississippi and South Carolina hundreds of acres, worn out from cotton cultivation, have been producing loblolly pine forests for several decades. In cycles of twenty years or so, sections of these pine forests have been harvested.

For all his interest in agriculture, particularly forestry, Clark was faced with a dilemma. "I had to make a decision," he declared in an interview. "Are you going to be a professor or a farmer?" After moving to Lexington he thought seriously about living on a Bluegrass farm, but even though Beth had grown up on a farm, she did not relish such a life. Ultimately, Clark had the best of both worlds. As a history professor he could not only teach and write about his beloved land but also, as a very active avocation, return the land to a more natural production than row crops.

Thoughout much of his academic career Clark has nurtured mountain land in Estill County, with soil, climate, and terrain different from his native Mississippi or South Carolina. On Barnes Mountain he bought land depleted by overtillage of corn by several generations of mountain farmers. Clark maintains it is the "best land in the country for producing hardwood trees." Again he practiced conservation, permitting the forest to return at its own pace. "You can't fight that mountain," he said. "Let the land have its head. It'll do right by you." The important lesson is to allow the land to go through natural stages of reforestation, where it will finally produce species of oak, tulip poplar, hickory, and maple. He proposes that much of Eastern Kentucky should be allowed to return to forests. And if the forests are properly managed, he argues, then trees should also be processed in Kentucky, rather than sending them by the truckload to furniture and manufacturing plants outside the state.

Like a true agrarian, Clark finds solace in his Kentucky mountain forest, a peace that only the husbandman can know. "When things get too much for me in this room [his study], I can go up there and forget the world."

Agriculture also encourages cooperation among neighboring farmers, a union that is often missing in today's mobile, materialist society. Even if the small farmer does not own much, he has a profound sense of independence. As one of poet James Still's mountaineer's proudly proclaimed: "I own this land, hell deep and heaven high."

Clark is an agrarian without being an advocate of agrarianism. He knew some of the Vanderbilt Agrarians in the 1930s, including John Crowe Ransome, Robert Penn Warren, and Allen Tate, members of a group of southerners who argued that modern urban life was destroying the traditions and vitality of the agriculturally based South. Clark found their philosophy wanting because most lacked firsthand knowledge of southern agriculture. "In one respect, farming is the most independent way of life we've ever had in America," but "you are also tied to economic forces you have no control over," he stated. Then there are the vagaries of weather and climate, which can destroy a season's work in a moment.

The agrarian world is changing today, with thousands of acres being abandoned. "Take those old barns," Clark observed. "They stare at you like old men gradually sinking into the ground." While he laments the loss of the small family farm, as an agrarian realist he knows the old days are gone.

Clark's philosophy lies somewhere between the agrarianism of Wendell Berry and the views of the enormous agribusinesses. Modern agrarianism does not admit to the drudgery inherent in farming. "Farm life is really hard and people need to understand that," Clark asserted. "I can share his dream," Clark said of Berry, but as an agrarian realist he does not believe a return to small farms will prevail. "I have the same love of the land that Wendell Berry has," he maintained. "I practice on a little bigger scale than Wendell does." Greatly admiring Berry as a writer, Clark claims that only "our applications are different." On the other hand, he laments the growth of factory farming by the agribusiness giants, particularly the production of chickens and turkeys that is so evident in the modern South. But, Clark admits that landowners who also work at other jobs, including factories, will survive as typical small farmers in the increasingly complex economic world of the twenty-first century.

True to his concern for the land and for history, during the 2000 meeting of the Kentucky General Assembly he supported the authorization of a Kentucky natural history museum, which will be funded when better times return to the commonwealth.

From the persistent march of the boll weevil across Mississippi to the continuing decline of tobacco culture in Kentucky, Thomas D. Clark has seen nearly a century of agricultural flux. From intemperate clear-cutting of ancient forests to the advent of a new century of conservation, he has seen much change. Nevertheless, it is his optimism for the future that challenges us all to conserve our forests and land.

For all his many accomplishments, Clark said with a grin at the conclusion of our last interview: "I'm nothing but a country boy, that's all, that's all I claim to be." He has not only kept us aware of the historical significance of change, but, as an agrarian realist, he has disabused us of our wanton misuse of our natural heritage.

Note

1. I have interviewed Clark on several occasions as part of the Kentucky Historians Oral History Project at Eastern Kentucky University. Unless otherwise noted, all of the quotations are from this series.

Education Advocate

Robert F. Sexton

Thomas D. Clark and his old friend, Yale historian C. Vann Woodward, corresponded for many years about their profession, their families, and the condition of the world. In one letter, though, Woodward groused a little too much for Clark, writing about the "miserable century" they had both lived through. "I don't share that point of view at all," responded Clark, "we can look back on this century and, I think, call it Kentucky's century."[1] Tom, perhaps more than any Kentuckian, knows the reality of Kentucky's historical problems with education. But he's an optimist anyway. This contradiction lies at the heart of his personal story and the appeal of his advocacy.

On Tom Clark's bedroom wall are two large color photographs of the Tallaheaga Creek in Winston County, Mississippi, near his birthplace. "That's where I walked in," he says, pointing to the top photo. Pointing to the other one, he adds, "That's where I walked out two years later." The pictures help tell the story of a pivotal turning point in his life.

It was not foreordained that Tom Clark would even receive a formal education, much less become a walking monument to Kentucky intellectual life. He could just as easily have gone the route of backbreaking labor on a Delta cotton plantation, like most of the young people he grew up with in Winston County. A former classmate, now a successful lawyer, wrote to him recently: "You know, it's a miracle. We were just a bunch of ignorant country boys."

What made the miracle possible, what pushed Clark toward education, was a teacher mother, determination, and good luck. As a child he attended the one-room schoolhouse where his mother taught. He's not sure what level he reached—maybe fifth grade. And he isn't certain where he learned to read, at home or at school. "They kind of blended together," he said.

The hardest times came when he was about fourteen years old in the dry depression summer of 1919. His father's cotton was being "eaten to nothing" by boll weevils. "Somebody had to do something to make some money." "What to do" appeared to him as he walked home from church one day with his parents and brothers and sisters. A distant whistle near the Tallahega Creek caught his attention. "What's that?" he asked his father. "They're dredging a canal," he answered. Tom left home the next morning to work and live on that dredge.

Two years later, "I simply got to the point that I realized that the rest of my life was going to be muddy and greasy, and I walked away on a rainy night. I walked through the swamp and got to my grandmother's house." Two days later he walked on to Mississippi Technical College, presented himself as a student, and was rudely rejected. "They lost themselves a student," he chuckles. But he kept on. "With each step, I became more aware that education was the magic ingredient that separated you from being just an ordinary, stumbling-around human being with limited knowledge and limited perspective."

Walking back home, the rebuffed Tom Clark stopped to see a family friend who ran a little restaurant near the train station. "He told me to get on the train and go to this town and see T.A. Patterson who ran an academy there." That's what he did. (There were no public high schools as we know them in Mississippi at that time.)

Tom's education began—and his luck turned around—when he stepped down from the train in Weir, Mississippi, and T.A. Patterson was one of two men he saw standing on the platform. "I told him I wanted to enter school," Clark recalls. "He never asked me one damn word about what preparation you had, what background or anything. He looked me over. . . . I was much heavier than I am now, and I'd been on that boat and pretty muscular. And he asked me if I played football. I never had heard of football. I'd never seen one. He looked me over again and he said, 'Well, you're a big stout boy, and we need some football players.'"

Thus began the academic career of Thomas D. Clark, football player and student at Choctaw County Agricultural High School. "I headed to the ninth grade. Monday I went out for football. Friday I played the first game. Four years I played football for that school." But he studied, too. And he "fell into the hands of Miss Ruby O'Quinn, a drop-out from Mississippi State College for Women" who taught elocution, and "she hammered on me, teaching me public speaking. . . . It got me in a mess the rest of my life," he says.

When Clark finished school four years and four football seasons later, he had become a member of one of the most elite groups in Mississippi—high school graduates—who numbered only about 10 percent of the adult population in 1920. When he traveled the next year to Oxford and the University of Mississippi, and later to the University of Kentucky and Duke University for graduate work, he joined an even more elite group.

The muddy and greasy struggle out of the Tallaheaga Creek ditch, the push from his mother, and the luck of finding a football-loving school superintendent distinguished Tom from the vast majority of young men in Mississippi or later in his adopted Kentucky. He knew full well what he had, he knew about obstacles to education, he knew that it wasn't easy, and he knew his advantages and lucky breaks. So he had a special sympathy for the boys and girls he met at the University of Kentucky in the 1930s. The young students who came to his classes there "had no idea," he says, "no preparation." The university had virtually no admission requirements except that students had to have completed about sixteen high school credits. "One boy appeared," he said, "with only fifteen credits, but said he had raised a prize sow in a 4-H program. 'Give the old sow credit and let the boy in,'" said the director of admissions.

When Clark got to the University of Kentucky, he "realized I had just stepped back into an environment that I had left. With inadequate education, every aspect of life of this state reflected lack of educational and material development." As a professor "you were only doing about a fourth of your job because you had to cut through so much handicapping. . . . Thank God I had understanding of what they went through." There were also great rewards, like seeing "these people bloom and flower" when they were exposed to good teaching and challenging course work.

Knowing that education didn't come easily, he believed college was not a lark but serious business. "I didn't have any sympathy for those slackers who had no reason to do anything but get out of bed. Sometimes I was pretty rough on them." He tells of writing to one boy's father, to the chagrin of his "scaredy-cat" dean, and telling him he was wasting his money and his son's time at the university. His dean was panicked. "We'll be sued," he whimpered. But, Tom says proudly, the father wrote back thanking him, saying it was the first time anyone at the university had given him straight information.

"You couldn't help but be interested in education," he says, especially after that first experience teaching in a state "so backwards and isolated." The "root problem in Kentucky and Mississippi"—the culture as he calls it—"was that people accepted the fourth grade as the upper level. Enough to be able to figure a little, enough to write, certainly to write a letter of some sort, and to read, at least to read a county paper. And that's about all they aspired to. The argument was that 'You don't need no education to plow a mule.'"

Sometimes I think I'm the only adult in the commonwealth who did not take Tom Clark's history class at the University of Kentucky. I was growing up in Kentucky while he was teaching here, but left the state for college and graduate school long before I met him. It was two thousand miles west, in Seattle, where we first got together. We met when I walked into his University of Washington classroom as his teaching assistant. He was a visiting professor there in the summer of 1968; I was in the last year of my doctoral studies in history. Because I planned to write about Kentucky history and would soon return home to do my research, I was anxious to get acquainted with the famous southern historian. Tom, meanwhile, had retired from the University of Kentucky and had just moved to Indiana University. For him, teaching in Seattle was a summer diversion, the kind of visiting professor stint he had enjoyed throughout his academic career. For me it was the beginning of a thirty-four-year friendship.

For his West Coast students of the 1960s Tom was an amazing and novel figure—a stately sixty-five-year-old in a dark suit, courtly and somewhat formal. The class he taught was on southern history. Through his lectures—accent, elocution, and all—his students could feel the suffocating Mississippi summer sun, or taste the fear of a destroyed cotton crop, or mourn the hopelessness of illiteracy. The South's neglect of education was a constant theme.

Eventually we both returned to Kentucky, and our lives and interests intertwined regularly. He was always ready for a crusade if it had to do with history, archives, or education. When I wanted (in the 1970s) to publish the papers of each Kentucky governor, I recruited Tom Clark to chair the first editorial board. When it was time to revise the state constitution (as it often was), he was there to talk about how to do it. When we decided to create a public policy think tank in 1987, Tom served as a founder. When people wanted the Shakertown Roundtable to concentrate on education, he helped plead the case.

We also came to be connected by the Prichard Committee. He was an early volunteer member of this citizens' advocacy group, an extended family of like-minded education advocates. He religiously attends meetings and even travels the state to exhort the faithful or convert the skeptics. Beyond our common work on education and other projects, my wife, Pam, and I see Tom and his wife, Loretta, often. Some of our favorite times with them have been driving to his forests in Estill County and hiking through his woods.

So Tom Clark is a fellow education advocate, a fellow historian, and a friend, neighbor, and traveling companion. It's in that personal spirit that these reflections about his role as an advocate for improved education are written.

About the time Tom Clark first set foot in Kentucky "fresh out of the cotton fields of the lower south," *The Nation* magazine published a lengthy article, "Kentucky: Where Men Die Standing," by journalist Ben Lucien Burman of Covington. Today's readers would see Burman's 1928 story as a quaint period piece, abundant with predictable stereotypes: fast horses, beautiful women, illiterate tobacco farming hillbillies, and, most of all, violent rifle-toting mountaineers. But I suspect that young Professor Clark took to heart Burman's concluding line: "This is the State's sin: life is too cheap. Let the Kentuckian barter his revolver for a book, and die in bed."[2]

In one way or another, Tom Clark spent the next seventy years trying to accomplish Burman's wish that books and reading would replace violence and ignorance in the Bluegrass State. A core fact of

Clark's public life was that he wrote, talked, exhorted, and worried about education in the South and Kentucky for his entire career. First and foremost, he was a historian. So we begin with his histories to understand what he thought about education.

Before Tom Clark was known as a Kentucky historian, he was a "southern historian." And education in the South and crusades to improve it were a constant in his research and writing. It is no accident that he entitled the published version of his Lamar Memorial Lectures *Three Paths to the Modern South: Education, Agriculture, and Conservation*. His view of education in the South paralleled his view of Kentucky, and his themes were remarkably consistent over seventy years. "Education," he wrote in the Lamar Lectures, "was the only means by which the South could elevate itself above the bogs of ignorance, poverty and economic enslavement." He had no sympathy for "nostalgic Southerners" who hoped for a second coming of the glories of an agrarian way of life. Such romantic dreaming, he thought, perversely distracted a region that was "bogged in debt, poor health, low personal efficiency, and deep personal frustration."[4]

Better schools were the only way out. "Delay in maturing an adequate public educational program revealed itself in many forms of failure, not least of which was stifling racial confusion, loss of population, ineffective labor forces, and Southern inability to compete economically with the rest of the country. Southern pride suffered enormous damage." The only hope for the future, he stressed, lay in "thousands of crusaders" who "presaged a South moving toward the national norm."[5]

These themes persisted as Clark wrote about Kentucky, which he saw as part of the South. He pulled no punches. He served up comments and interpretations readily. He told his readers where Kentucky should go, not just where it had been. He praised education crusades and crusaders. He blasted the "intellectual snaggers who considered

Kentucky's educational deficiencies a heaven-mandated condition."[6] He bounced between hopefulness and despair as he thought of prospects for the future. In his writings between 1940 and 1970 he wasn't encouraged by what he saw in Kentucky's past or current leaders. It was in one of his books, for instance, that I first read *Louisville Times* editor Tom Wallace's famous quip. When asked, "Who runs Kentucky?" he answered: "It doesn't run—it limps."[7]

Looking at Kentucky history, Clark decried the dead weight of the past. "Education was Kentucky's cross," he wrote in *Kentucky: Land of Contrast*. "It was difficult indeed to persuade a self-satisfied rural population to act when it was unschooled, afraid of taxes, wedded to the idea that to raise more money for public purposes only served the interests of venal officials, and, finally, convinced that what was good enough for the past generations was good enough for the future."[8] Indignation prevails; his language has more vinegar than sugar. His passion and outrage leap out. He is even harsh, some might say. Blunt descriptions lace his pages: "escaping barbarism," "vast social inertia and selfishness," "little men grasping for power," and "a state of economic and cultural stupefaction."

In his mind, a "deep rooted agrarianism" was the primary barrier for Kentuckians as they floundered to enter the modern economy. For him the pejorative terms "agrarianism" and "social inertness" weren't necessarily rural conditions, they were more a pervasive state of mind ingrained in the culture of the commonwealth. "From the banker on Fourth Street in Louisville to the corn-patch farmer at the head of Barren River, the Kentucky mind was cast in the same cautious negative mold of conservative countrymen. For them no adventure should be undertaken which endured beyond the span of a single crop season."[9]

Where did this culture come from? From the way Kentucky was settled, who the first settlers were, what they thought, and how they survived. Kentucky's culture developed through the immediate practicalities that mattered most to the pioneers. Survival was fundamental; subsistence farming, timbering, and hunting were the ways one survived. Big families were popular because they created the "labor force to operate a subsistence farm, clear the land, do the heavy work." Labor-intensive extractive pursuits left little time for school; as laborers, childrens' strong backs paid off more than trained minds.

National origin and religion also helped form the culture. The thousands of Scottish, Irish, and English pioneers who struggled over the Cumberland Gap or flat-boated down the Ohio River "didn't bring a love of education in their baggage and were not from the educated classes." Later, when the Erie Canal opened, a new wave of immigrants moved westward, "dodging slave territory" and heading toward Illinois, Ohio, Minnesota, Wisconsin and other states that today we see as rich in education. These immigrants—German, Dutch, Swiss, French, Scandinavian—established public school systems as soon as they settled, unlike the Kentucky settlers. Religious preferences were a factor too, Clark argues, in that the Baptist preachers predominant in Kentucky often "boasted that they were illiterate and that they were moved by the spirit, not by the word, and certainly not the word of man."

Throughout the 1800s and into the 1900s the world around Kentucky and the South changed. "Joining the growing industrial and commercial world"—or just keeping up—became the state's challenge. The pace accelerated until World War I saw the "old modes of life altered if not destroyed." Behind in education from the start, Kentucky and the South began the process of catching up, a struggle that would continue from the 1850s to the present day.[10]

His clear-eyed review of the state's history notwithstanding, Tom saw much reason for optimism in his research. He saw great promise in the stories of past advocates, or "crusaders" as he called them, for improved education. He admired the "whirlwind campaign" for schools in 1908 and, before that, the reform movements of the 1840s. Both failed, he writes, from loss of momentum or hostile circumstances such as the Civil War. He also saw much to be hopeful about in the 1949 Commission on Kentucky. He sounded his most positive note as he concluded his comprehensive *History of Kentucky*: "Perhaps the most concrete fact in Kentucky history at mid-twentieth century was that a large body of thinking citizens had become aroused to the ever-expanding demand for public services."[11]

But his worries about the future also persisted; he expressed them in his last major Kentucky history, *Kentucky: Land of Contrast*, in 1968. As he gave them voice in that book, Tom previewed the themes and the rhetoric that would dominate Kentucky's political conversation for the next thirty-five years.

> No longer can Kentucky politicians and educators orate
> their state into a condition of economic and cultural stupe-
> faction and have it remain happy and prosperous. People
> will have to be fairly well educated just to hold a common-
> place job, no matter in which part of the state they now live.
> . . . The new industry shows a remarkable lack of apprecia-
> tion for the delights of anticipating the opening of squirrel
> hunting season or the fact that fish are biting in the creeks
> and lakes. For the first time in Kentucky history the state's
> leadership is being told that it must deliver something more
> tangible than glib political promises and faithless perfor-
> mances if Kentucky is to keep abreast of its competitive
> neighbors.[12]

As the last decade of the twentieth century dawned, Tom was involved in planning the future of the Prichard Committee. His old hope that "thinking citizens" would bring about school improvement in 1950 had been dashed, he said in a letter to committee chair Wade Mountz. Still, he was optimistic again because the Kentucky Education Reform Act had been enacted, "one of the truly great landmarks in Kentucky history. . . . Kentucky has now just begun to accomplish the conduct of an effective and efficient educational plan."[13] But he was also worried. "In former crusades good laws were enacted, but the public groups that brought about their passage either [lost] interest or assumed they had accomplished their objectives, with the result that there was never a full realization of the dream."[14]

History shows, he said, that the critical challenge and the way to avoid past failures was to keep momentum alive, a task he envisioned for the Prichard Committee and for himself. "What I would shout to you, and to the Prichard Committee [is] . . . don't let your momentum die. And don't let that old line, narrow-minded, illiterate, ignorant, cussed element in the state tinker . . . with KERA, ever. Now KERA itself has to keep its face clean and it's got to pump new ideas, new vigor. If it doesn't, it's a gone cause."

Such assertiveness for advancing an education reform agenda grew from the scholarship of Tom Clark the historian. When he took to the stump, as he did more and more after retirement, he was also driven by his optimistic nature. Despite all the problems he identified, he also said that "Never and never and never any moment in my life did I think educational improvement . . . couldn't be accomplished." Thus armed, he became a public citizen in the mold of the crusaders he admired so much.

Most Kentuckians know Tom Clark as the commonwealth's head storyteller, its teacher-at-large. There are no records of exactly how many talks he has given or of how many people have been in his audiences in the past decades, but a safe guess would be thousands of events and hundreds of thousands of people. He is our own unique walking, talking museum, my wife, Pam Sexton, says. His incomparable skills are enlarged because he collects not only books, stamps, horseshoes, and trees, but stories and lore and friends—friends like Anthony "Ticky" Smith and Doodlebug McKinney, who help with his Estill County forests and his forty-year-old pickup truck. He puts his knowledge and his life together, Pam says, "like one of those museum boxes filled with recorded information: You walk up and push the button, and his stories flow out—a gift to all listeners."

He is revered because he makes history personal, and people relate not only to his story but to him. He always teaches, always tells and explains, whether his audience is the Prichard Committee, a television interviewer, a governor, or a hiking companion. His capabilities, Pam says, are so strong because they are so integrated into his life. The things he knows and cares about aren't in separate boxes. His advocacy is so much a part of him that it becomes almost invisible, blending in with the background, like the trees in his forests. But the teacher, the storyteller, is rarely quiet. His life's work has been and still is making linkages among the events of the past and the present and the possibilities of the future.

Recently Tom and Loretta Clark and I drove out of Lexington for Middlesboro before dawn on an October Saturday so the storyteller could weave his magic at the dedication of the newly reconstructed Cumberland Gap trail. People in the area love their ninety-nine-year-old friend. Five years before, he spoke to them when the new Cumberland Gap tunnel opened. Tom and fellow historian John Mark Faragher star in the Park Service's promotional video. And the park superintendent had also asked him to tour the new trail before it officially opened to the public; when we got back inside after that damp, foggy day in the woods, Tom said that seeing the Wilderness Road that way had been a highlight of his life.

The trek obviously inspired his speech at the official dedication ceremony. He spoke without notes and with his usual eloquence and color to a cold but happy band of dignitaries, costumed historical re-enactors, and local history buffs. The emotional scene found Tom standing square on the Great Warriors' Path as it descended into Kentucky. The attentive crowd saw a sage from another world. His words created a picture that they could see along with him as he spoke of the "endless procession" coming out of the forest and down the trail with a "gleam in their eye, of that great dream of an Eden that lay beyond—anticipating fortunes and futures and dreams that lay beyond the Gap itself.[15]

What he did that day was a metaphor for his contribution to education in Kentucky. He reached people and captivated them with a vision of their ancestors' dreams and their struggles to realize them. He fashioned a span of words, speaking out a story that connected his modern audience to its past, building a bridge for them that spanned 250 years and then moved into the future.

"Sunrise in Kentucky" is what Tom Clark called the passage of the Kentucky Education Reform Act in 1990. That's where his bridge led. "We're almost in the presence of a miracle," he said, "the crowning moment of the century."[16] Twelve years later he was still optimistic. "Kentucky has . . . made greater progress in education advancement during the past decade than in any comparable time in its history."[17]

Tom, though, liked to put things in their larger perspective. A few years after the Kentucky Education Reform Act was passed by the legislature he said, "I don't think we need to use the term 'reform' any more. I think we are past that stage. I think we understand very clearly that we need to . . . constantly make changes . . . that we say to ourselves if we are going to keep the educational system timely, keep it in synch with the time, with the changes, with the demands which are sure with us at the moment and most certainly will be a major central challenge of the next century."[18]

But he also worried about roadblocks he had seen for six decades: "lack of vision and statesmanship," "politicians who failed to provide adequate financial resources," "stifling bi-partisan bickering," and fears of "reforming Kentucky's archaic revenue system as if it were the black hole of Calcutta." The result—an inadequate state budget— would be, he warned in 2002, "disastrously frustrating and costly, and [would] give the cold shoulder to the fundamental needs of Kentucky."[19]

When he spoke of Kentucky's 1990 reform, he was most interested in the vision behind it and in its potential, not the details and nuances of this complex public policy. No one was better at speaking for the lofty aspirations, the grand vision that Kentucky could rise above the burden of its history he had described so often. His faith in the 1990 reform and his other opinions about education grew from core beliefs that are consistently woven through his career's writings:

- *A belief in the power and obligation and leadership to cause positive change.* The leadership he admires is willing to make hard decisions, to invest resources in the future, and is able to rise above "regional and partisan inhibitions." In other words, it is the opposite of what he deplores in history—"venal," "selfish," "weak," "regional," "backward" leaders.
- *A view of education as an investment and tool to help individuals live better lives and to make Kentucky a better, more prosperous place to live.* He is a historian and a humanist, and he values academic pursuits as worthy in themselves. But when he talks of public education, practical language overrides romance every time.
- *An uncompromising, tough mind.* Education cannot be im-

proved or attained by an individual without effort. The frustrating thread that runs throughout our political history, he says often, is that politicians have grasped for ways to improve schools painlessly. The settlers who came through the Cumberland Gap "did not bring with them in their cultural baggage a zeal for education. And when they did get around to it, they undertook to do what Kentuckians are still trying to do—trying to build an educational system as painlessly as possible."[20]

- *A focus on the need for a plan.* The chief failure of Kentucky's past political leadership, his published histories show, was going two hundred years without a "plan." A plan in his view is a way to turn political rhetoric that "orates Kentuckians into stupefaction" into something that makes a difference.

- *A belief that spending on public services is an investment, not a cost, and that funding schools and universities is the most important investment of all.* Support for schoolteachers and professors, coupled with rigorous and high expectations, tops his list of priorities.

- *An optimism about the future, despite tough criticism.* His messages are always filled with hope, his political instincts (a characterization he would disavow) having told him that true leadership requires finding solutions for the problem you've told people they have. In his later years, this hopeful spirit, combined with his gift for storytelling and his venerable age, give him immense persuasive power.

I expect it was his optimistic spirit that led Tom to admire crusaders like those who pushed progressive reforms in the post–Civil War South or who led the Commission for Kentucky in the 1940s. The failure of the Commission for Kentucky was a disappointment, but he never gave up. "There's a lesson in these past failures for the

Prichard Committee and most of all for the people," he said. "Don't let the momentum die."

Thomas D. Clark has faith in education as an institution and in its potential for bettering individuals and society. He believes that education can be improved with a good plan, good political leadership, popular support, adequate financial resources, and talented and well-educated people teaching in schools. The "miracle" he saw in the 1990s was that these things had come together in Kentucky's 1990 school reform.

But he also thought that it would take years to know if the "sunrise" he hoped he saw was real. "We have it in the law," he said in 1990, "but we don't have it in the classrooms yet." As the new century opened, he worried again that weak leadership would be Kentucky's limitation, repeating history by trying to build a strong education system "painlessly," without adequate taxes. The results might once more be "unrealized goals and opportunities" and the "cold shoulder to the fundamental needs of Kentucky."[21]

But his optimism prevailed again, and he wrote in 2002 that, despite the state's financial blight, there is "still time for statesmanship. . . . The chief gainers," he exhorted, "will be the state's populace and its public institutions. In an era when civilization itself faces such drastic challenges, the state cannot afford to waver."[22]

I expect that his hope-filled visions of well-educated Kentuckians and genuine statesmanship were akin to those he saw in that "endless procession" of men, women, and children coming through the Cumberland Gap, anticipating their "fortunes and futures and dreams" that lay beyond. As far as Tom Clark is concerned, I'll wager, we are all still part of that procession.

NOTES

1. Author interview with Thomas D. Clark, Lexington, Ky., Oct. 28, 2002. Quotations not otherwise indicated are from this interview.

2. *Nation,* [date?], 149.

3. Thomas D. Clark, *Three Paths to the Modern South: Education, Agriculture, and Conservation,* Eugenia Dorothy Blount Lamar Memorial Lectures, No. 8 (Athens: Univ. of Georgia Press, 1965), xi.

4. Ibid., xi-xii.

5. Thomas D. Clark, "Birthday Toast for Robert F. Sexton," Midway, Ky., Jan. 13, 2002, text in possession of the author.

6. Thomas D. Clark, *Kentucky: Land of Contrast* (New York: Harper and Row, 1968), 264.

7. Ibid., 236-37.

8. Ibid., 238.

9. Ibid., 245.

10. Thomas D. Clark, *A History of Kentucky* (Lexington, Ky.: John Bradford Press, 1954), 442.

11. Clark, *Kentucky: Land of Contrast,* 287.

12. Thomas D. Clark, "Prichard Committee 20th Anniversary Comments," July 9, 2000, Cumberland Falls State Resort Park (text in possession of the author); Thomas D. Clark to Wade Mountz, March 28, 1990.

13. Clark to Mountz.

14. Thomas D. Clark, "Dedication of Cumberland Gap Trail," Oct. 19, 2002 (transcript in possession of the author).

15. "Historian Thomas Clark Views Education Reform as 'Sunrise in Kentucky,'" *Lexington Herald-Leader,* April 1, 1990., A2.

16. Thomas D. Clark, "Education Can't Afford State Budget Fight," *Lexington Herald-Leader,* June 21, 2002, A13; Thomas D. Clark, "We Still Have a Long Way to Go," *Kentucky Monthly,* Jan. 2000, 56.

17. Thomas D. Clark et al., "Lessons from the 20th Century: Historians and Younger Leaders Talk about Kentucky," Shakertown Roundtable Discussion, Nov. 5, 1997.

18. Clark, "Education Can't Afford State Budget Fight." A20. Thomas D. Clark, "Education: A Bridge to the Future," Prichard Committee Conference, Nov. 17, 1987 (transcript in possession of the author).

19. Thomas D. Clark, "Historian Thomas Clark Views Education Re-

form as 'Sunrise in Kentucky,'" Lexington *Herald-Leader,* June 21, 2002, p. A13.

20. Clark, "Education Can't Afford State Budget Fight."

Kentuckian

JOHN ED PEARCE

The term Kentuckian covers a multitude of identities. It is not easy to say with certainty just who is a Kentuckian, or why. Most people considered or claiming to be Kentuckians are those who are born in the state, live within its borders all or most of their lives, are buried in its soil. But there are others who also may claim or deserve the title. Some are born here but leave to find careers or broader horizons but never cease to think of themselves as Kentuckians. Some live their lives outside the Bluegrass state but, by their own design, are brought back to be buried in the soil of their beginnings. Others—and they, perhaps, deserve the name just as much—come from places outside to find in the commonwealth something that speaks to them of home, the end of searching. Some come with industrial or business firms, meaning to stay only until promotion or change of fortune draws them away, but find in time the feeling of belonging.

Lexington especially has a talent for attracting people and making them captive to its peculiar allure, an atmosphere that is neither exclusively southern nor northern but a casual blend, an air of northern cosmopolitan energy with an undercurrent of relaxed southern charm. No matter what one's cultural tastes, beliefs, religion, or political philosophy, he can find in Lexington kindred souls. The town owes much of its personality to the University of Kentucky, to which young people are drawn from across the state and from other regions and who stay or return, perhaps in hopes of prolonging the richness of youth or simply because they found there a lifestyle that suited.

And now and then, though not too often, a person will come to Kentucky and find not only that the place has become part of him but that he has become part of it. He need not forsake his roots in other places or discard the tender memories of years before he came. He may not even intend to remain, but life moves and he with it, and in time he finds that he has arrived at the place where he was meant to be.

Such a man is Tom Clark, Dr. Thomas Dionysius Clark, whose life sprang from the rich soil of the Mississippi Delta and who found meaning in the rich limestone earth of the Kentucky Bluegrass. It was chance and the early signs of his abilities that brought him here, that and the search of a young graduate in history for a post where he could do what he wanted—to teach history to others.

That is what he has done. Legions of Kentuckians say, as did a former governor recently, "Of all the professors I had at the University, the one who most influenced my life was Dr. Clark." He taught from a wellspring of enthusiasm, hoping to inculcate in the young minds before him the respect and love he had for his subject. Though his specialty was Kentucky history, his teaching was not limited to the land within the commonwealth borders. As the history of Kentucky is part of the story of mankind, so did he regard his students as individuals taking part in the vast sweep of the history of America and of the world. Such subjects were worth studying and understanding because they were the story of humanity, in all its majesty and failings. He sought to send his students forth realizing that they shared the human spark.

Which is not to say that he was a man given to professorial gravity, though he was possessed of the dignity that came with confidence in himself and competence in his calling. He was, and is, a man of unfailing humor. In the classroom he mixed jokes and human-interest stories into his investigation of history. Former students, as well as his congregation of friends and admirers, speak of his unfailing smile, the humorous tilt of his head, as well as the determined energy that marks his movements as he heads toward his century year. To put it simply, Tom Clark is an admirable and likeable man, the more so not only for what he is and has been but for what he has given.

It is significant that his talent was recognized early on by Dr. Frank LeRond McVey, president of the University of Kentucky, whose dedication to the academic enrichment of the university won for him a lasting place in the annals of the school. McVey personally approached the young Memphis University teacher and offered him a place on the University of Kentucky faculty. It proved to be a natural match of man and place. Clark was immediately popular with both students and fellow faculty members. In 1942 he was named chairman of the Department of History and began assembling a distinguished history faculty. For generations of students, his name became synonymous with the University of Kentucky.

He did not limit his energies and inquiring mind to the campus. Soon after he came to Lexington he began to explore the state, to familiarize himself with its people, its topography, its folklore and legends and history. He traveled across the state, visiting courthouses, coal mines, one-room schools, and roadside stores, country post offices, bus stations, remote hollows, farmland, and mountains. He explored the rivers that lace the state, noting their effect on the culture and economy of the towns along their banks. In his travels he began to sense the tenor and fabric of his adopted state, and this yielded a double benefit. His increasing interest in and knowledge of the state added a dimension and a flavor to his classroom lectures, and they fanned the creative spark that resulted in a series of books about Kentucky, including a history of the state that is still the standard by which other histories are measured.

Gradually he immersed himself in his adopted state. He became part of it, and it became an inextricable part of him. One result was a succession of books about Kentucky towns and counties, rivers, roads, and railroads. He became known as the premier voice of and for Kentucky. He was named Historian Laureate. The name Tom Clark became synonymous with Kentucky.

But there remained, and still remains, in Clark a quiet strain of the southerner, reflecting a boyhood spent among the cotton fields and lumber camps of his native Mississippi, as well as a literary tone reminiscent of the rich cultural heritage of Oxford. His travels included long voyages into the South; he earned his doctorate at North Carolina's Duke University, and the extensive list of books he has authored includes histories of the South and its nature through the stages of its change.

But at heart, as well as in residence, Clark is a Kentuckian in the true sense of a man who has immersed himself in the state and its culture and become in turn a part of its spirit. He has been a citizen of the state in every sense of the word, involving himself in a broad range of public affairs. He has campaigned for an improved state constitution. With a love of nature stemming from his boyhood, he has been active in and an outspoken advocate of conservation. He has appeared before the Urban Council and before legislative committees of the General Assembly to lobby for laws affecting education at all levels, and he has not hesitated to express his opinions on matters affecting the University of Kentucky, including the acts of its trustees and the selection of its leaders. He has supported expansion of the university but has insisted on the importance of faculty over physical construction.

There is irony in the fact that during an era that most reflected his enthusiasm for academic excellence, Clark experienced the single critical setback he suffered as a university professor. It occurred during the presidency of Dr. John Oswald, whose policies and drive for academic improvement at first won Clark's support and enthusiasm. But as part of his effort to upgrade the faculty and to attract to the campus young, energetic minds, Oswald deemed it necessary to shake up the various departments, and this entailed replacement of several department heads. Rather than appear to be demoting selective individuals, Oswald adopted a policy of rotating departmental chairmanships. And one of the chairmen was Clark. Significantly, when he left the university, Oswald is reported to have said that the one decision he regretted most during his tenure was "that I rotated Tom Clark."

The incident did not, however, dim Clark's devotion to teaching and the field of history. He had been too active for too long in too many fields, there was too much juice left in the man, too much appetite for life simply to quit when he retired from the University of Kentucky in 1968. Nor did he have to. In recognition of his talent, he was recruited to teach at Indiana University, and while there produced a multivolume history of that institution. But, after retiring from IU in 1973 as Distinguished Service Professor Emeritus, he came back home, teaching history for a while at Eastern Kentucky University and entering again into the civic and cultural life of the Bluegrass. It was during this period that he wrote his history of agrarian Kentucky and the history of Laurel County.

Time has dealt kindly with Tom Clark. In a ceremony in his honor at Ashland, the home of Henry Clay, a speaker pointed out that Clark regarded time not as an enemy or obstacle but as an opportunity. No dry academician, he takes a personal interest and an active part in the political life of the state, never hesitating to offer his opinion of the people involved in it.

Above all, Clark is indefatigable. He simply refuses to surrender to age. In October 2002, as he approached his hundredth birthday, he was honored in the state capital with a ceremony hailing publication of his massive book, *The People's House: The Governor's Mansions of Kentucky*, an exhaustive and beautiful work that he coauthored with Margaret A. Lane of the Kentucky Historical Society, and which he views, with some justification, as the apex of his productive career. His interest in and concern for his state has never flagged. He is active as well in the civic life of Lexington. It is worth noting that in his ninety-ninth year he has been tireless in the campaign to persuade Lexingtonians to purchase control of their water company, arguing for the wisdom of keeping Kentucky control over the water resources that will so basically affect the future lives of Kentuckians.

Nor has his taste for and enjoyment of life diminished. After losing his wife of more than fifty years, he remarried in 1998, and he and his wife, the former Loretta Gilliam Brock, enjoy a full social life that would be exhausting to a much younger man. He enjoys an afternoon at Keeneland, an athletic event at UK. He attends civic luncheons, benefits, and official ceremonies—and speaks at many of them—as well as frequent functions held in his honor. Thomas D. Clark's name has become familiar to all segments of Kentucky, and he is recognized not only as the state's senior historian but as its premier citizen. He has not only taught Kentucky history but has emblazoned his name indelibly on its pages. He has become a symbol of what is meant by the term Kentuckian.

Preservationist

WILLIAM MARSHALL

A phone call awakened Thomas D. Clark at three o'clock one early spring morning in 1936. James W. Martin, Clark's University of Kentucky colleague, who also served as the Commissioner of Revenue in Governor A.B. "Happy" Chandler's administration, quickly explained the reason for the call. The previous day the state librarian had sent two truckloads of state records to Louisville to be sold as scrap paper, and more were to be sent that morning. "I want you to go to Frankfort with me," Martin hurriedly told Clark. "Don't take time to dress, just go as you are."[1] Throwing on his clothes over his pajamas, Clark joined Martin for the drive to Frankfort. Arriving at the west end of the state capitol building, they spotted two trucks loaded with state documents. Martin rushed next door to the governor's mansion to awaken Happy Chandler. In the meantime, Clark attempted to prevent the departure of the trucks.

When told of the scheme, Chandler became livid and directed Martin to inform the contractor that the governor would have him thrown into the penitentiary if he did not unload those two trucks and return the loads already sent to Louisville. Meanwhile, Clark encountered the state librarian, Mrs. Ethel G. Cantrill, as she was involved in a heated discussion with the contractor over Clark's effort to stop the trucks. As she gazed at Clark, the state librarian recognized him. "Who told you that?" she asked the contractor. And, looking at

Clark, he said, "He did." "Well, I'm sunk," she replied.[2] The core of the state's archives escaped destruction. More than two dozen truckloads of material were eventually removed to the basement of the University of Kentucky's Memorial Hall, where they were to remain until a proper facility could be located or constructed.[3]

Thomas D. Clark has been the steward of Kentucky's history for more than seven decades. Preserving primary source materials for research and other uses is one of his passions. Influenced by his mother's interest in history and his Uncle Pink's intriguing Civil War stories, Clark spurned possible legal and medical careers to court the mysteries of Clio. Following undergraduate work at the University of Mississippi, in 1928 the young man, after a coin flip, chose to pursue a master's degree at the University of Kentucky rather than the University of Cincinnati. Clark's work on Kentucky's postwar trade with the South familiarized him with the commonwealth's meager libraries, including the University of Kentucky's limited holdings. As a result of his travels, UK president Frank McVey, who had become a father figure to Clark, hired him through the history department to survey seven central Kentucky libraries in search of materials that would support a doctoral program in American history. His two summers of work (1929, 1930) yielded a compilation of 1,282 book titles and 126 newspaper listings.

Clark's interest in the use of primary source materials heightened as he researched antebellum southern railways for his doctoral dissertation at Duke University under the tutelage of professor William K. Boyd. In addition, he was also exposed to the ideas of D.W. Connor, the University of North Carolina history professor who in 1931 became the Archivist of the United States.

The young historian was also influenced by the activities of J.G. de Roulhac Hamilton (1878-1961), the historian who founded the Southern Historical Collection at the University of North Carolina.

Hamilton envisioned a historical repository where scholars and researchers could come to study the history of the American South. As a part-time field agent, Hamilton scoured the South for manuscript collections. His collecting success earned him the nickname "Ransack" Hamilton. Opened in 1930, the Southern Historical Collection contained more than two million pieces by the time of Hamilton's retirement in 1948 and today remains the preeminent repository for the study of southern history.

Spring 1931, in the midst of the Depression, found Clark desperate for a job. He approached University of Kentucky president McVey, but the young historian was unsure that the history department had any openings. In the meantime an instructor's position opened at the university in political science and Clark was hired—only to be quickly fired when the chair of the department discovered that, though his work was completed, the young historian had not actually received his degree. By April 1931 McVey hired Clark to teach in the history department and collect materials to support the history graduate program.

Since its founding, the university had struggled with limited financial support. Clark later recalled, "The university looked shabby . . . it operated on pretty limited resources. . . [and] the staff was small."[4] The University's meager library holdings were divided between a tiny Carnegie building and the administration building, which held a reference collection. Fortunately a new library building was begun in 1929 and completed two years later. Aside from President McVey, little internal support could be found for Clark's collecting activities. He remembers that history department head Edward Tuthill "couldn't have given a damn less about adding to the library. He was no way in favor of me doing that work and did some very mean things to throw blocks in the way."[5] Indeed, Tuthill attempted to cut Clark's salary and assigned him a full load of classes to hinder his collecting.

Moreover, Clark's support from the library was lukewarm at best. Although she accepted his activities like "a good soldier," the university's librarian, Margaret I. King, "never saw the importance of establishing a research library."[6] While valedictorian of her UK graduating class in 1898, King's focus for an academic library was primarily "getting books to students, running a good loan desk, [and] building a good reference department."[7] Nevertheless, King accompanied Clark on numerous trips to collect resources, and when other members of her staff did not want to get "their hands dirty. . . Miss King plowed in and got the job done."[8] Clark still likes to recall the time two people peered out the window at a truck full of incoming archival documents. When one asked what was in the truck, the other replied, "Oh, that's just some more of Dr. Clark's junk."

Nevertheless, in spite of the Depression, limited resources, and less than unanimous support, Clark embarked on a great adventure. His travels through the state took him everywhere. "I traveled over this state about every way that a man could travel," he recalled, "from riding a mule to walking, in a canoe, in old trucks and cars. It was pretty rugged getting around in parts of Kentucky in those days."[9] There were still many fascinating Kentuckians to become acquainted with who had once played prominent roles in the commonwealth's history—politicians like A.O. Stanley and Urey Woodson, and women's rights activists like Laura Clay. In addition, the thousands of people he met while teaching extension courses—an activity necessitated by the university's poor salaries—proved to be even more important connections. While the prospect of donating personal papers to the university library delighted most Kentuckians, a few viewed the institution with disdain. Some middle- or upper-class families who sent their sons and daughters out of state to school expressed little respect for the university's fledgling graduate programs.

Tips that Clark obtained in casual conversation often became the chief means of locating materials. One such tip netted the Burley To-bacco Cooperative's records stored in an old barn. In another instance, when former University of Kentucky professor and Centre College president Charles P. Turck learned that Clark was gathering research materials, he offered the college's collection of government documents to the university. It was taking up badly needed space in the college li-brary and was of little use to the undergraduates. President Turck re-ceived praise from the *Louisville Courier-Journal* for his gesture but faced criticism from members of Centre's Board of Trustees for his generosity.

Early in the 1930s, Clark received word that a large segment of the Durrett Collection still remained in Louisville. For years Kentuck-ians had lamented the fact that amateur historian Lyman Draper had come through the state late in the nineteenth century gathering his-torical materials that were eventually donated to the Wisconsin His-torical Society. Another archival setback occurred when Louisville his-torian Reuben T. Durrett sold his outstanding Kentuckiana collection to the University of Chicago. Excited by the prospect of finding much of the collection still intact, Clark went to Louisville to visit the fam-ily member who owned it. Although he was invited into the house, agitation within the family prevented Clark from looking at the col-lection. Undaunted, the young historian returned again, only to be faced with a similar situation. Told by the apparent heir to the collec-tion that he could have whatever he wanted, Clark returned the next day and filled two trucks with material out of the estate's carriage house. As he loaded the collection, the heir and another man unex-pectedly appeared through a big board fence. Clark could tell that the heir had no idea who he was. After the historian introduced himself, the man said, "Oh, well that's all right, just go ahead, take the stuff."[10] Afterward, the man's companion explained the confusion as he told Clark that they had just returned from a funeral and that it was the first time in a long time that the heir had been sober.

The persuasive collector was not always convincing enough to bring home his quarry—especially when he dealt with the Louisville and Nashville Railroad, a large company with secrets to protect. Railroads have always captivated Clark, particularly their relationship to the opening of the American West—the so-called "great land grab" wherein the railroads manipulated Congress, state legislatures, and the courts. After completion of his first book, *The Beginning of the L&N* (1933), Clark repeatedly lobbied with the Louisville and Nashville Railroad to open their records. Even his acquaintance with the line's presidents and legal counsel failed to yield results. During certain periods of the state's history the L&N "owned the Kentucky legislature, lock, stock, and barrel," recalled Clark. "They didn't want prying historians to come in and see how they owned it. They had attorneys in counties where they had not an inch of railroad. They had attorneys there for one reason—to make sure that the local legislators didn't vote against their legislation."[11] Moreover, they remained sensitive about their role in the 1900 assassination of Governor William Goebel.

Clark's most extensive collecting venture began almost innocently during 1942, the first full year of World War II. The funding source for an approved sabbatical leave to write a book on poor whites fell through, and the historian could not cancel his arrangements because the history department had already hired someone to take his place. Left to support a wife and two young children on half-pay, Clark arranged for his family to stay in South Carolina with his understanding in-laws. He then set out with a box of note paper and a plan to study the role of country stores in the South.

He planned to talk to country store owners about their businesses and make copious notes from their records. At his first stop he found the store's records stacked on the floor in obviously neglected piles. The store's proprietor confessed to Clark that he was about to throw the old ledgers away and that he could take them if he wished. Clark wasted no time loading his car and went on to the next store, where he achieved the same result. With no more thoughts of taking notes, "every time I went into a store I would go and look around before I would introduce myself," he remembered. "I got to where I could spot the records quickly. And then I talked to the merchant and I would say, 'I've been picking up these things. They are of no use to other merchants, would you part with [your] records?' And, they would agree right off."[12]

Clark's carloads of ledgers, account books, and business documents became the key to his next publication. Moreover, there is little likelihood that few if any of these records would be preserved today without Clark's efforts. The country stores in cotton country not only provided their customers with everything they needed from tools and machinery to clothing, seeds, and canned goods, but functioned as de facto banks for the cotton farmers. Therefore their ledgers and records not only recorded routine financial transactions but also provided extremely insightful information on a customer's loan and credit status and overall financial well-being. Over several months, Clark developed a collecting pattern based on time and geography that took him through portions of North Carolina, South Carolina, Georgia, Alabama, Mississippi, Louisiana, western Tennessee, and Kentucky, where he gathered records from more than forty businesses. "I cannot tell you the dust that I must have swallowed digging those records out," he recalled.[13] He also had numerous adventures with his Dodge burdened with heavy loads on weak wartime tires.

The son of a cotton farmer himself, the opportunistic Clark had little difficulty talking most storeowners out of their records. He would chat with a proprietor for a while and gradually explain to them who he was. "I knew the language," he recalled. "They quickly found out I wasn't some jaybird drifting around all over the South."[14]

Clark faced resistance on only a few occasions. In Huston, Georgia, a storeowner was very dubious of Clark and told the traveling professor that he wanted to keep his records. Desperate to establish his credibility, Clark retrieved a copy of the mortgage on his home from his car and showed it to the man. The storeowner examined it and, exposing the basis for his suspicion, exclaimed, "Good God! A man that deep in debt can't be a revenue officer."[15]

In another instance, in Faunsdale, Alabama, one of the heirs to the Brown family's mercantile operation made a deal with Clark. "You can have the records on one condition," she said. "That you get over there and pack them up and get out of town because there is a corpse coming in on the train and there will be a great gathering at the depot and I'd rather you wouldn't be around at that time."[16] Acting with great dispatch, Clark hired two young men to help him pack up the records and take them to the railroad freight depot to be shipped to Margaret King at the University of Kentucky. The historian recalled driving over the railroad tracks that afternoon just as he heard the whistle of the train bearing the casket approaching the station. The Brown records proved to be an outstanding resource—the family ran a cotton gin, a fertilizer business, and a really good general store in Faunsdale. Clark's collecting adventures during 1942-43 eventually led to the publication of his book *Pills, Petticoats, and Plows* (1944). The work quickly became one of the young historian's most ingenious, humorous, and popular publications. Moreover, his innovative and ground-breaking use of primary sources to document the southern country store achieved well-deserved recognition in the historical profession.[17]

Clark's historical activities also drew him into a close relationship with the staff of the Filson Club, Louisville's private historical society. Founded in 1884, the club maintained an excellent speaker's series at which Clark became an annual fixture during the 1930s, 1940s, and

1950s. The Filson Club was also the home of Kentucky's most extensive holdings of privately generated historic documents—a collection that is still painstakingly cataloged item by item. Unfortunately the club did not have space for large volumes of material, nor was it philosophically prepared to take on the records of large business firms. This was the situation faced by Ludie Kinkead, the Filson Club's curator, in 1944 when she learned that J.P. Morton Publishing Company was going out of business and that the building housing its records had been sold. The new owner contracted with a local paper company to sell the firm's records for scrap—a very profitable business because of the wartime scarcity of paper. The owner told Kinkead that the club could have whatever it wanted before the scrap dealer took possession of the records.

Not realizing the university's interest in such collections, Kinkead contacted several out-of-state institutions, including the Harvard Business School, the University of Chicago, and Vanderbilt University. None of them were interested. It was only by a stroke of luck that Clark learned of the situation from one of his colleagues at Vanderbilt the weekend before the records were to change hands. The J.P. Morton Company was one of the preeminent southern publishing houses during the nineteenth century, and the Kentucky historian knew that saving the firm's records would be a research coup. In a race to beat the next day's deadline, Clark arose at 3:00 a.m., took a truck to Louisville on a Sunday, and worked all day long in a grimy basement to extract material. Clark later wrote to the director of libraries at Vanderbilt, "We fought the scrap people all the way down the line but, luckily, we got out with all the records."[18]

Clark and his family were particularly close to Otto Rothert, the popular secretary of the Filson Club (1919-46). At Clark's invitation, "Uncle Otto" occasionally attended meetings in Lexington of the Book Thieves club—a group of men who gathered monthly to discuss books and areas of potential research, the location of valuable sources, to read each other's manuscripts and discuss stimulating ideas. Members of the group, most of whom were successful authors, included Clark; Lincoln expert William H. Townsend; Charles Staples, an authority on Lexington history; Dr. John S. Chambers, who wrote on cholera; gentleman farmer J. Winston Coleman, who authored numerous works including *Slavery Times in Kentucky*; UK president Frank McVey; physician Claude Trapp; and the group's convener, Judge Samuel M. Wilson, the owner of a fabulous Americana and Kentuckiana collection.

According to Clark, the handsome, white-haired Wilson "had keen eyes, bushy eyebrows, and was always chewing on an unlighted cigar. An eloquent speaker with a slight rattle in his voice, he had the memory of an elephant—the presence of an iron man."[19] Wilson was an indefatigable researcher who would acquire any book or resource available so that he had all of the research at hand. There were times when his acquisitiveness strained the family budget and caused Mrs. Mary Shelby Wilson to admonish him. Judge Wilson also held a formal annual gathering of what he called The Cakes and Ales Club, ostensibly to celebrate Washington's birthday. What he really wanted to do was to examine some of the rarities he asked his guests to bring. Partially as a result of the strong friendship that developed between Clark and Wilson, the latter willed his collection to the University of Kentucky and Clark became one of the coexecutors of his estate.[20]

In 1946, not long after Wilson died, Clark went through the judge's Mentelle Park home and his downtown office and found books and manuscripts everywhere. Wilson, who had participated in one of the Goebel trials, had previously told the historian that the secret of who assassinated Governor William Goebel in 1900 was located in a quilt box at his home, but Clark found no such evidence. Nevertheless, the collection was a literal research gold mine that contained more than 10,000 volumes including many rare books, 100 cubic feet of manuscripts and archival material, pamphlets, photographs, public documents, the remains of the judge's research, and fifty years of correspondence. Judge Wilson's gift was the "seed" collection that provided UK with a firm research foundation and finally persuaded the university to develop a Special Collections unit in addition to its institutional archives.[21] The Wilson Papers were dedicated on April 1, 1951, with Luther Evans, the Librarian of Congress, giving the keynote address.

As Clark's administrative responsibilities at UK and his professional commitments increased, he found less time to collect material. To keep the momentum going he successfully lobbied to have a member of the history department, Dr. Bennett Wall, hired as a part-time field agent.[22] In the history department's 1954-55 Annual Report, Clark praised Wall's efforts, scolded Kentucky's citizens for being reckless with the state's history and leaving the burden of collecting it to the university, and noted that the history department "could not pretend to do advance work in the field of history without an adequate manuscript collection."[23] He articulated his position further as he stated:

> Collecting historical materials goes far beyond any practical utilitarian purpose of writing theses and dissertations. Not until we have these materials collected can we be certain that a valid interpretation can be made of Kentucky and regional society. Now I believe we can be on the way to making a beginning in this direction. Kentucky has desperate need for more mature interpretation than has been given it in the past. Thus the collection of a large body of papers and records which may appear as dust-catching trash to the unsophisticated is of the utmost importance to the people

of the state. These are the laboratory materials of all the social sciences and humanities. There is a tendency at times to believe that a trained historian with a textbook in his hand and a crowded classroom of students before him is all that is necessary to convey a concept of the past in a meaningful way for the future. This is one of the most damaging myths which has been allowed to grow in the academic garden.[24]

At the same time Clark was continuing to build UK's collection, he was utilizing his national ties in the historical profession. In 1951 he persuaded Philip Hamer, executive director of the fledgling National Historical Publications Commission, that the University of Kentucky was the logical place to headquarter an edited version of the Henry Clay Papers. With Hamer's encouragement, Clark received funding from UK's Research Committee and hired staff, including professors James F. Hopkins and Mary Wilma Hargreaves, to locate Clay material and initiate the project. By early 1952, Clark had not heard from the NHPC and wrote Hamer that to "secure" the "research fund now in hand it is necessary for me to act in a hurry."[25] Then, in a desperate tone he added, "If it is necessary to get the support of the Kentucky delegation in Congress, I stand right ready to do that, but as I told you, we mean business about the Clay Papers but we have to have support from the outside." To Clark's relief, Hamer and the NHPC provided outside funding. No one, including Clark, realized how long such historical editing projects would take to complete. The common wisdom of the time was three to four years. After forty years of editing and expenditures totaling more than $2 million, the Clay Papers project produced ten volumes plus a supplement and completed its work in 1992.

With the Clay Papers editing project launched and the university's

Special Collections firmly ensconced in the library, one would think that much of Clark's work was completed. Such was not the case. The professor's wide-ranging research, teaching, professional, and administrative responsibilities or interests failed to keep him from being constantly entwined in the fate of the state's public archives.

Not long after he and James W. Martin made their early morning dash to save the state archives from the scrap paper dealer in 1936, Clark ordered literally tons of records removed from the statehouse to the basement of Memorial Hall, where WPA employees worked on them. Logistically, the move did not always progress smoothly. The university had only two trucks for this duty—a half-ton vehicle called the "new truck" and an old rubber-tired Dodge truck. The men moving the records overloaded the Dodge truck on one of the trips and it "reared up" on the hill at the Woodford/Fayette County line on U.S. Route 60 and tumbled through a fence, where it overturned in a cow pasture. Records were scattered everywhere. The supervisor of the operation called Clark and pleaded with him to leave the records where they were. Tom Clark's reply was "Hell, no!!!"[26] The soiled, wind-blown records were duly retrieved and taken to Memorial Hall.

The status of Kentucky's public records was tenuous from the beginning. With the exception of its land records, which it dutifully promised Virginia in 1792 that it would maintain, there was no provision for keeping records. According to Clark, most states were "just as careless as drunken sailors" when it came to being responsible for their records. "I can't think of a worse state than Kentucky—you couldn't have been any worse than Kentucky if you had set out willfully to mismanage records. . . . Yet, I stand back with open-mouth amazement that as many records survive. What we don't know is how many records were lost."[27]

The concept of scheduling records was a foreign idea in the 1940s and 1950s, but when some state agencies learned of the University of

Kentucky's trusteeship over the state's records, other record groups, like those of the state's court system, were also sent to UK. In another instance, Ward Oates of the Kentucky Department of Revenue wrote Clark in 1941 that his department had between twenty-five and forty file drawers filled with reports from retail liquor licensees covering purchases between 1936 and 1939. "We probably will never get around to using the reports for statistical purposes," he wrote, "but the thought occurred to me that some of the people at the University might find them useful."[28] In 1948 the Court of Appeals records and the state archives were moved to the King Library. In the late 1950s, after Clark was named chair of the state's first Archives Commission, he was asked to look at a roomful of records being held by the State Highway Commission. Upon examining the material, he quickly realized that they were worthless toll bridge tickets that had been torn in two. "The state was spending an enormous amount of money to take care of that trash," he recalled. "Well, we cleared that room out in five minutes, because it had no value of any sort."[29]

Clark's lobbying and personal leadership were behind the 1958 law that mandated the preservation of Kentucky's public records and the formation of a state agency to regulate and care for them. The state passed a model law, which was highly praised in professional archival circles, creating a state archives. Unfortunately, during the State Reorganization Act of 1962, the Kentucky legislature tinkered with archives law without realizing the full impact of their actions. The damage done by the new legislation took several years to repair.

Another difficulty arose because of the conviction of George Chinn, the director of the Kentucky Historical Society, that the archives should be part of his organization. Chinn called a meeting of the board of the Historical Society, of which Clark was a member, to discuss the matter. Clark incurred Chinn's "anger forevermore and intentionally and militantly so" by refusing to yield to the director's

scheme.[30] Clark did not want the two organizations combined because of the Historical Society's public/private status and because he
knew the archives would be swallowed by the Historical Society's ge-
nealogical mission. "We had quite a hair pulling," he recalled, "and I
won."[31] Dr. Clark was reunited with Kentucky Historical Society activities soon after General William Buster became director in 1973
and was named a member of the Executive Committee in 1982. In
addition, Clark was named as one of the original members of the
Kentucky Oral History Commission in 1976—an organization now
part of the Historical Society. His counsel and leadership in that body
contributed greatly to the success of Commission-sponsored oral history projects throughout the state.

Constructing a suitable repository to house the state's archives and
records proved to be a career-long challenge for Clark. Beginning with
the Ruby Laffoon administration in the early 1930s, Clark lobbied
every governor for a building to hold the state's archives. In the 1940s
he went to see Governor Keen Johnson, who sat and looked at Clark
and said, "I'd be glad to support a building, but we don't have any
money." "Well," recalled Clark, "Keen was just as stingy as he could
be and [he] admitted his stinginess. We weren't about to get a building."[32] Six governors later, Clark went to Governor Louie Nunn's
commissioner of finance, who promised to give the archives a building. The commissioner sent Clark out to look at an old former tex-
tile mill on property owned by the state located on a creek close to
the old penitentiary. The old three-story building was full of broken
windows—glass was everywhere and the site was a royal mess. The
historian became so angered that the state would even suggest the location as an option that he sent a heated letter rejecting the site and
suggested that the state might as well burn the records. The commissioner of finance told Clark, "That's the roughest letter I've ever gotten." Clark replied, "I meant for it to be rough. Somebody has to get

rough with the state. We're losing records. We are acting like total illiterates—just totally irresponsible in the handling of the state's records."[33]

As the 1970s dawned and the state archives continued to grow, the agency clearly needed a separate building. The archives shared its headquarters with the State Library at Berry Hill—an old Frankfort mansion. Its holdings were stored in five different buildings at three separate locations. Archives users, who were not numerous, were served by a single reference archivist in a tiny research room that was part of a leased warehouse located behind a grocery store off US route 60 in Frankfort.

During the Wendell Ford administration, the 1974-76 budget contained a $3 million appropriation for a state library building to be constructed. But the project was tabled over the state library's inability to define its role, and the funds mysteriously evaporated into other portions of the budget. Finally, in 1975, with Julian Carroll's election to office, Clark had a former student in the governor's chair. He wrote to Carroll noting that we "desperately need" a building for the State Library and Archives. Moreover, he stated, "We get little or no publicity, the press passes us by, and people out in the State scarcely know we exist, but when it comes to investigating the past the archives are indispensable." [34] Carroll sent Clark to study existing buildings to see if they would be suitable for the archives. After a string of fruitless inspections, however, Clark wrote Carroll again and suggested that we are "nowhere" and that we should either "get in or get out of the archives business." Carroll replied with a handwritten note, "I'll give you the building."[35]

The state legislature appropriated $10 million for the building, to be constructed on a twenty-eight-acre site at the old state farm. Clark and other state employees accompanied architects on visits to examine leading archival repositories in several states. When the bids were opened, much to the relief of Clark and others, most were under budget. The state negotiated a contract with the winning bidder and authorized a construction order. Governor Carroll broke ground for the building on his last day in office, in December 1979, and Clark proclaimed that "this is one of the proudest days of my life."[36]

Almost immediately, however, unforeseen circumstances threatened to derail the building. As John Y. Brown Jr. assumed the governorship, the Carter administration cut off federal funds to the states, forcing the new administration to find a way to operate state government without them. All building projects were halted. In late January Clark went to Brown's office to argue in favor of continuing the building project. Instead, he was ushered into the office of Don Mills, the governor's executive assistant. Mills, who had also been a student of Clark's, quickly confirmed that Governor Brown did indeed want to discontinue the building project, but that the contractor wanted $3 million to get out of the contract. Fearing criticism from The *Louisville Courier-Journal* and a loss of funds with nothing to show for it, Mills informed Clark that the project would continue. It was a close call.

The building, which was dedicated on October 8, 1982, became a beacon light for researchers. Its three-story-tall lobby is graced by a massive free-standing wooden sculpture, which has the appearance of a huge jigsaw puzzle in the shape of the Commonwealth of Kentucky. Created by Murray, Kentucky, sculptor Bobby Reed Falwell, the pieces of the composition are carved from assorted native woods donated by Clark from his tree farms. The rendering is a unifying form representing the assemblage of Kentucky's vast and disparate archival holdings and certainly Clark's role in that process. The nearby research room attracts thousands of visitors each year from across North America.

The facility, now filled to capacity, currently holds 146,000 cubic feet of archives and records. The building has become a catalyst for other activities as public archivists and representatives from other states visit the facility. In addition, it has motivated the Kentucky Department of Libraries and Archives staff to play a more prominent role in regional archival groups, such as the Southeastern Archives and Records Conference (SARC), and to build a network of relationships with fellow archivists in other states. Moreover, the building provides Kentucky's citizens with a visible definition of archives. They cannot fail to be impressed with miles of shelving stocked with records and a reference room filled with microfilm readers and friendly reference archivists waiting to assist them. Finally, the building sends the message that the commonwealth is able to exert its legal authority and stewardship over its records. It signals county clerks and judges, the administrative officials of the courts, the state's institutions of higher learning, and other state officials in Frankfort that the state is serious about caring for its past and that they should be too.

Clark's participation in the life of the Kentucky Department of Libraries and Archives steadily increased in the 1980s. He is a key member of the state's Archives Commission as well as a member of its Local Records and Advisory Boards. His forty-four-year tenure on the Archives Commission has provided the archives with a continuity and leadership unparalleled in most institutions. As Richard Belding, the state's Archivist, notes, "His membership has really helped to bring new members into a much better understanding of what the responsibility of a commission member is. They have a unique mandate to identify what records will be destroyed, what records will be retained, and that they are essentially the custodians of history in the sense of selectors of that documentation from which history will be written from this period. If they make a wrong decision, that will have consequences that we really cannot appreciate at this stage."[37]

In 1983 Clark became one of the founders of the Friends of Kentucky Public Archives—an organization formed to assist the Kentucky Department of Libraries and Archives in safeguarding the state's heritage. During the following year he spoke before a joint session of the state legislature as an advocate for legislation on the local records program. Legislative members, many of whom were his former students, listened with rapt attention and respect as Clark spoke with authority and passion on the issue. "The doing of it," noted Richard Belding, "had an effect that would have been unmatched by any other person I can think of."[38] The Local Records Act passed and has provided for the preservation of thousands of unique documents, ledgers, and record books in local courthouses and other entities.[39]

In 1985 the Friends of the Kentucky Public Archives created an endowment fund in honor of Clark to provide archival apprenticeships for graduate students seeking archival careers. Finally, in 1992 Clark received the J. Franklin Jameson Award for archival advocacy from the Society of American Archivists. The award is given to a person who is not an archivist but who is a principal supporter of the profession. According to Richard Belding, Clark "is the perfect example of what the profile of a winner should be. He never was an active archivist in any sense, but he could not be more interested in the work of manuscript curators and archivists and people who have that responsibility."[40]

During the 1990s Clark's advocacy continued. In 1999 the Kentucky Historical Society completed a badly needed History Center and Museum. Clark, a long-time Executive Board member of the society, worked quietly behind the scenes to sway legislators in support of the project. He also worked tirelessly to raise money from such donors as the Toyota Corporation.

As we leave the twentieth century behind us, Clark continues to produce book-long manuscripts on his manual typewriter. Although he does not use a personal computer himself, he is aware of the importance of electronic records and the difficulties and costs inherent in preserving them. As a member of the Archives Commission he still battles with those concerns and issues on a monthly basis.

Clark has been an untiring and almost fearless supporter of the preservation of archives and history for nearly three-quarters of a century. Never one to worry about soiling a good suit, Clark is an inveterate collector who is willing to search out the historical record himself in closets, basements, attics, or even haylofts and chicken coops. He has traveled to the remotest reaches of the state and on rare occasions has put himself in precarious situations. On a rainy day in the 1930s, for instance, he traveled by mule to visit a country store not far from Sandy Hook in Elliott County. On his return trip he encountered a boy with an umbrella on a very narrow, slick, and rocky stretch of road. The mule, which was laden with saddle bags filled with store records, refused to budge at the sight of the umbrella. Clark persuaded the boy to put down his umbrella and leave the scene. Only then was Clark able to coax the mule over the slippery rock. On his return to Sandy Hook, he "wondered where [his] head was."[41]

As an author, Clark immersed himself in the historical record. Unlike some of his colleagues, Clark's books provide testament to his work in archival repositories and libraries. As Richard Belding noted, "Clark uses the records that we hold. He talks to the staff on how he is using them and they save the products of his research and the books he publishes."[42]

The longevity of Thomas D. Clark's advocacy on behalf of the state's public and privately generated historical archives, records, and manuscripts over the past seven decades is truly amazing. His work at the University of Kentucky spawned and helped maintain the institution's Special Collections and Archives unit—the state's most extensive collection of privately generated primary source material. He secured funding to initiate and maintain the Henry Clay Papers editing project during its first two decades. In addition, he assisted in locating the funding and political support needed to create the Kentucky Historical Society's new History Center in 1997. Moreover, he literally saved the state's public archives from destruction in 1936, he is directly responsible for the creation of the Kentucky state archives through the passage of a model archives law in 1958, and after almost fifty years of lobbying he succeeded in persuading state government to provide the archives with a modern building. Finally, he has influenced the lives and careers of countless historians, archivists, and librarians and has earned their undying respect. In so doing, he has certainly earned the sobriquet "The Steward of Kentucky History."

NOTES

1. Thomas D. Clark interview with William Marshall, Dec. 10, 2002, Special Collections and Archives, University of Kentucky Libraries (hereafter cited as Alumni-Faculty Oral History Project).

2. Ibid.

3. The state's records were officially given to the University of Kentucky by Governor Albert B. Chandler. Minutes of the Meeting of the Executive Committee of the University of Kentucky, Tuesday, June 16, 1936, 1-2.

4. Thomas D. Clark, interviews with Terry Birdwhistell, May 6, 1981, Alumni-Faculty Oral History Project.

5. Ibid.

6. Ibid.

7. Ibid.

8. Ibid.

9. Ibid.

10. Ibid.

11. Thomas D. Clark presentation, Archives and Manuscripts Management (LIS 643) class, University of Kentucky, spring 1984 (hereafter cited as Clark Archives class presentation, 1984).

12. Thomas D. Clark interview with James Giesen, July 10, 2002, Alumni-Faculty Oral History Project.

13. Clark interview with Marshall, Dec. 10, 2002.

14. Clark interview with Giesen, July 10, 2002.

15. Ibid.

16. Clark interview with Marshall, Dec. 10, 2002.

17. Two dissertations, both by archivists, Jacqueline Page Bull and Lewis Bellardo, were also based on these records.

18. Thomas D. Clark to Dr. A.F. Kuhlman, Lexington, March 29, 1943, Clark Papers, Box 1, Activities—Library—Correspondence, 1935-1945, University Archive and Records Program, Special Collections and Archives, University of Kentucky Libraries.

19. Clark interview with Terry Birdwhistell, April 21, 1986, Alumni-Faculty Oral History Project.

20. Others included Clinton M. Harbison, J. Winston Coleman, and William H. Townsend.

21. A case for funding support was made to President Herman Donovan by the university librarian, the chair of the history department, and the director, bureau Source Materials in Higher Education, on Aug 10, 1945. Clark Papers, Box 1, Activities-Library-Correspondence, 1935-1945.

22. Subsequent field agents included F. Gerald Ham, Herbert Finch, and Charles Atcher.

23. Clark Papers, Box 17, History Department, Annual Reports, 1950-57.

24. Ibid.

25. Thomas D. Clark to Philip Hamer, Jan. 17, 1952, Clark Papers, Box 1, Activities—Henry Clay Project, 1951-1952.

26. Clark interview with Marshall, Dec. 10, 2002.

27. Clark Archives class presentation, 1984.

28. Clark Papers, Box 1, Activities—Library—Correspondence, 1935-1945.

29. Clark Archives class presentation, 1984.

30. Clark interview with Marshall, Dec. 10, 2002.

31. Ibid.

32. Clark archives class presentation, 1984.

33. Ibid.

34. Thomas D. Clark to Julian Carroll, Sept. 17, 1975, Clark Papers, Box 245, Correspondence Series: Carroll, Julian—Carter, H.

35. Clark interview with Marshall, Dec. 10, 2002.

36. Clark Papers, Box 245, Correspondence Series: Carroll, Julian–Carter, H.

37. Richard Belding interview with William Marshall, Dec. 4, 2002, Alumni-Faculty Oral History Project.

38. Ibid.

39. House Bill 26 provided for a standardized marriage form. Part of the cost of the form and transaction was used for the preservation of records through the Local Records Program.

40. Belding interview with Marshall, Dec. 4, 2002.

41. Clark interview with Marshall, Dec. 10, 2002.

42. Belding interview with Marshall, Dec. 4, 2002.

Publisher

WM. JEROME CROUCH

It was indeed an auspicious moment for the University of Kentucky, for Kentucky itself, and for scholarly publishing in the commonwealth when in September of 1928 the westbound Chesapeake & Ohio train bearing Thomas D. Clark pulled into the station at Lexington, even though the band and the crowd on the platform were there to greet Clark's fellow passenger, Senator Charles Curtis, the Republican candidate for the vice presidency. Fittingly, like many of the settlers who had preceded him into the state that he was to claim as his own, Clark arrived in Kentucky by way of Virginia, where he had attended the summer session at the university in Charlottesville. Like them, too, he came to Kentucky pursuing a dream—to further his aim of becoming a professional historian by working toward a master's degree at the University of Kentucky.

The university was then led by President Frank L. McVey, himself a scholar, who had the vision of transforming a complacent and provincial institution into a forward-looking one with a faculty animated by scholarship and research. Publication, for McVey, was a necessary part of any research effort, and as early as 1917 he had put forward the idea of a university press as having an appropriate role in the purpose of a university. Two years later he established a monograph publishing fund administered by a faculty committee.

In the small world of the Kentucky campus, Thomas D. Clark

soon caught the eye of President McVey. Older and more mature than other students, Clark must have impressed McVey with his energy, enthusiasm, and obvious dedication to his work. Doubtless, McVey saw in him the potential for research and scholarly endeavor that he wished to encourage in the faculty. When Clark finished his master's degree after one year and left Lexington to work on his doctorate at Duke University, McVey urged him to return to Kentucky after he had completed his residence requirements. And this Clark did in 1931.

The new instructor in the department of history not only carried the customary heavy teaching load of those days but also undertook, at McVey's request, to build up the library's holdings and to stimulate research and writing among his colleagues. In addition, McVey imbued Clark with his own enthusiasm for a university press at Kentucky, an enthusiasm that he maintained despite loss of the monograph fund to the exigencies of the Depression. Clark collaborated with McVey in order to keep the idea of a press alive among the university's faculty. Ever a visionary, even when there seemed no possibility of funding, McVey undertook a study of university presses in 1934, making personal visits to several of them. According to Clark, he was especially impressed by Bill Couch and his press at the University of North Carolina, which was a pioneer academic publisher in the South, but Couch was not at all encouraging. Nevertheless, McVey set up a faculty group, including Clark, to discuss the feasibility of a press.

During that same time Clark became an active member of the Book Thieves, to which he had been introduced by McVey. The Book Thieves were a group of professional men, all deeply interested in Kentucky history and in collecting books and manuscripts of Kentuckiana. The interests and talents of these men accorded well with Clark's own indefatigable canvassing of the state to build up the university library's collections, and besides, they made up a convivial gathering who enjoyed good food and good cheer. Often their after-dinner talk, no doubt steered by Clark, turned to the possibility of a press at the university and how it might come about. Like so many endeavors bruited during the lean years of the 1930s, nothing came of these informal discussions.

But a break in the financial constraints occurred in 1939 when Margaret Voorhies Haggin, widow of the millionaire horseman James Ben Ali Haggin, set up a trust fund at the University of Kentucky in honor of her husband. McVey immediately took advantage of this largesse by setting up an annual fund of $2,000 to be controlled by the Monograph Committee, now designated the Publications Committee, for the purpose of publishing monographs and other research projects of the faculty.

At some point about this time, Clark recalls, P.J. Conkwright, a young book designer for the Princeton University Press with close ties to Kentucky, approached him with the idea of reissuing some rare Kentucky titles to be edited by Clark and designed by himself. Wanting to see something come from the new Haggin funds and suspecting that the faculty was not going to be productive, Clark agreed to this proposal, and with a grant of $500 the Clark-Conkwright team brought out in 1940 the first of the Kentucky Reprints, *Festoons of Fancy* by William Littell, Esq. (1814). This book and two subsequent volumes that appeared in 1942 and 1945 were printed at the Princeton University Press, and all three won distinguished awards for their typography and design and brought favorable attention to the University of Kentucky's fledgling venture into publishing.

When McVey retired from the presidency of the university in 1943, he and Clark, then head of the department of history, together persuaded McVey's successor, Herman L. Donovan, to recommend to the Board of Trustees that it establish the University of Kentucky

Press. The board approved the recommendation at its meeting on September 21, and Donovan appointed a new University Press Committee with McVey continuing as its chair. Fittingly, Clark became a member of this committee and served on it until his retirement from the university in 1968.

With McVey now outside the university's administrative circles, Clark took over as the most active and consistent advocate of the new university press. From his vantage point as head of the history department he enlisted Wendell H. Stephenson, formerly the managing editor of the *Journal of Southern History*, to serve as professor of history as well as editor of the press. Stephenson, however, left after only one year with nothing to show for his tenure. Without delay, Clark in 1946 recruited another historian, J. Merton England, to replace Stephenson in the department and in the editorship of the Press. England had little more success as an editor than did Stephenson; Clark remembers that he edited only one book, a selection of poetry, *Tip Sams Again* (1947) by Cotton Noe, a university faculty member and Kentucky's first poet laureate.

Even though the new press possessed a formal name, it did not have a formal structure. Governance by committee members with no defined administrative responsibilites had produced no consistent aims or guidance and, more importantly, no identifiable progress in developing a publishing program. Nor had Clark's appointment of members of his department as part-time editors succeeded any better in focusing activity and encouraging publication by the faculty. The University of Kentucky Press appeared in real danger of foundering before it had set sail.

Once again it was Thomas D. Clark who took the initiative in seeking to advance the faltering program that had become his special care. Clark made the Press Committee and the administration face up to the situation of the Press. He pushed the university to decide ei-

ther to set the publishing program up as a formal agency or to aban-
don it altogether. By 1949 at his instigation the university did adopt
a comprehensive plan that would establish the University of Kentucky
Press as a separate agency under the president of the university, with
a full-time professional director and provision for hiring other professional staff.

Returning after lecturing at the University of Vienna, Clark discovered that in his absence nothing more had been done about the
press. Exasperated, he pushed for the hiring of a director. In the course
of publishing his Fleming Lectures at the Louisiana State University
Press, Clark had become acquainted with Bruce Denbo, who had edited his manuscript and whom Marcus Wilkerson of the Press had
recommended to him as a likely candidate for the Kentucky job. On
September 1, 1950, Denbo was hired, and the University of Kentucky
Press had its first full-time director.

Having set up a structure for the University Press, during the next
year Clark set about providing a charter for its operation. He and a
special committee of seven other senior faculty members worked out
a comprehensive publication policy to guide the Press. It was one of
the earliest such documents among American university presses. Near
the end of the decade another committee reevaluated that initial
policy. It found that there existed few avenues for publishing smaller
monographic works and recommended that the Press create what
came to be the University Studies Program under its own editor. It
also recommended that the Press reopen an earlier series, Studies in
Anthropology.

On a mundane level Clark had to wage a battle with the university administration over the question of printing the University Press's
books. An old law required that all material from state agencies had
to be handled by the state printer in Frankfort. Fortunately a more
recent act of the legislature had rescinded that requirement, but even

so the vice president of the university held out for the state printer. After several spirited meetings Clark finally won over President Herman Donovan to the idea that the Press could find other printers. Then another hurdle came from the School of Journalism, which wanted to insinuate itself into the operation until Clark personally intervened with the head of the school and persuaded him of the difference between publishing and printing. As a matter of fact, Bruce Denbo was hired with a dual responsibility—one as director of the University Press and the other as head of the university's printing plant—and for many years the Press's books were printed in that plant until it could no longer handle them in addition to its primary work of producing printed materials for the university.

In 1963 John W. Oswald became president of the university. Fresh from the vice presidency for administration on the Berkeley campus of the University of California, Oswald had large plans for the university—increasing the physical plant, emphasizing graduate programs, recruiting productive faculty, and requiring more research and publication. His plans called not only for the participation of the Press but also for an expansion of its program to meet these goals. In 1965 Clark was appointed to head the University Press Committee, and under his leadership the committee began a study of the Press and of its role in furthering President Oswald's aims. On his own, Clark had studied Kentucky's colleges and universities, for this was a time of change, with the state's five state colleges being elevated to the rank of regional universities. One feature of the Press Committee's new policy statement, based on Clark's findings, was a recommendation for a program that would lead to the transformation of the University Press into an agency that would serve all institutions of higher learning in the commonwealth—an idea indicative both of Clark's foresight and of his larger vision for the good of Kentucky as a whole.

As matters turned out, the issue of a statewide university press came up right on the heels of the Press Committee's latest review of publishing policies and prospects. And, it might be added, hardly a year before Thomas D. Clark's retirement from the University of Kentucky. As Clark remembers the time, he was reading the Sunday morning paper and came across a review of a book bearing the imprint of the Morehead State University Press. He immediately saw the appearance of this book as a presage of other such ventures. For him the growth of publishing agencies on other campuses across Kentucky, with its limited financial and intellectual resources, would result in a deplorable dilution of quality, an overall mediocrity that would reflect poorly on all the state's colleges and universities. He lost little time in seeking to create the statewide university press that he had envisioned earlier, a press that would be a natural extension of the University of Kentucky Press, which had already achieved national recognition for the quality of its books.

After reviewing the situation with the university administration and with Bruce Denbo, Clark called for a meeting of representatives from the state's public institutions as well as from some of its private ones to discuss the idea of a statewide publisher, what form this agency might take, and how such a cooperative venture might be set up. Later other meetings took place, including what appears to be the final one, held on the campus of Eastern Kentucky University in the spring of 1968. Initially there were reservations and objections all around—questions of control, of primacy, of financial commitments, of identity. Such deep reservations were hardly surprising, given the history of public higher education in Kentucky, where the institutions were more often than not "political" rivals, constantly vying with one another for financial support from the legislature and where the others all regarded the university in Lexington as their chief rival, always conniving to maintain its superiority over them.

To counter these objections and to provide an outside viewpoint and practical publishing background, the Press brought in Victor Reynolds to visit the campuses of the proposed members of the new agency and to discuss with their administrative officers questions they might have. Reynolds was at the time director of the University Press of Virginia, a cooperative publisher for Virginia's public universities, and had come to Virginia from a long-time directorship at the Cornell University Press. He was a senior leader in the field of American university press publishing and, moreover, he offered a hard-headed view of the business side of publishing, the problems and costs of creating and maintaining an effective operation. Undoubtedly his meetings and his subsequent report went far to make plain the invest-ment of funds and personnel required by a publisher, the benefits that could accrue from pooling resources rather than dispersing them, and, in the case of Virginia, the practical arrangements of a cooperative agency.

But everyone involved agrees that the decisive voice in the nego-tiations over the proposed new press was that of Thomas D. Clark. The prestige and good will from years of speaking across the length and breadth of the commonwealth, his perceived integrity, and his obvious concern for the whole of Kentucky—all these, probably more than other considerations, worked to sway presidents and their boards in favor of laying aside their rivalries and voting to establish the new University Press of Kentucky. Some have remarked, partly in jest, that it was the first time the state's public institutions had all cooperated on anything.

The new press was formally set up in March 1969 with an edito-rial board composed of representatives from all the member institu-tions. Founding members of the press were: Berea College, Centre College of Kentucky, Eastern Kentucky University, Kentucky State College (now Kentucky State University), Morehead State University, Murray State University, the University of Kentucky, the University of Louisville, and Western Kentucky University. Later the Filson Club (now the Filson Historical Society) and the Kentucky Historical Society became associate members, and Bellarmine College (now Bellarmine University), Georgetown College, Northern Kentucky State College (now Northern Kentucky University), and Transylvania University joined the consortium. It is the largest such consortium in the United States and, at the time of its founding, the only one to include both public and private institutions. Its founding might well be said to be the culmination of Thomas D. Clark's long espousal of publishing at the University of Kentucky and a fitting cap to his career at the university.

Though no longer an official member of the university, Clark has continued to offer support and encouragement to the program of the Press. Like other agencies, the Press since its earliest days has been constrained by limited funds to invest in new projects. Too, for the past several years the Press has had to rely more and more on its own resources to support itself and its program. This has meant that, especially with large and expensive projects, as much effort has had to be devoted to the search for funding as to the project itself. One of the goals set by Kenneth Cherry, who succeeded Bruce Denbo as director of the Press in 1978, was to create an endowment for the Press to meet the recurring need of support for publishing projects. Though they had commenced earlier, the efforts to create such an endowment became focused in the plans to publish a state encyclopedia. Philip Ardery of Louisville took the lead in this renewed effort and enlisted the support of leading businesspeople in the state. Clark gave his enthusiastic support to this endeavor, and when it was formally incorporated the members voted that it be named the Thomas D. Clark Foundation. Income from the foundation is now used for various projects, an example being the recent *Atlas of Kentucky*.

Clark did not limit his efforts to coaching from the sidelines or to running interference on the academic and administrative playing fields. At times he took a more direct role in the conception and actual creation of various projects. The first instance of such an editorial involvement was his collaboration with P.J. Conkwright in the publication of three rare items of Kentucky history that appeared in the very early days of the Press and brought it favorable notice. Another early project, one that became a monumental undertaking, was the publication of the papers of Kentucky's leading political figure, Henry Clay. This project had its beginnings in the late 1940s when Clark ran into an old friend, Philip Hamer, at a meeting of the American Historical Association. Hamer had recently been appointed the director of the National Historical Publications Commission, which was beginning to plan for the publication of the papers of the early political leaders of the United States. He asked Clark to see about the publication of Clay's papers. Agreeing to do so, Clark returned to Lexington to promote the idea. But it was not until the appointment of a full-time director at the Press that any progress was made. Shortly afterward James F. Hopkins, a professor of history at the university, was chosen to be the editor. The next step was funding. Clark and Bruce Denbo first approached the Greyhound Bus Company and Barry Bingham, owner of the *Louisville Courier-Journal*, and secured a small grant from each one. Then followed two visits to the Eli Lilly Foundation in Indiana that resulted in a substantial grant, letting the project proceed. The first volume appeared in 1959. Twenty-three years and four editors later, the eleventh and final volume was published. Reminiscing about this project, Clark said: "I look back on some things and wonder how we did it. Well, I'll tell you how . . . just by hard, bare-knuckle work. And I could not tell the time I put in on that project . . . without actually doing any of the work."[1]

Subsequently Clark became involved with a very different venture—*Kentucky: A Pictorial History*, released during the Christmas season of 1971. The notion of a popular book on Kentucky originated with Bruce Denbo, who like Clark was an adopted Kentuckian and who, possibly inspired by him, had taken the state and its colorful history to his heart. The task of being the overall editor was given to J. Winston Coleman, a well-known local historian and a friend of Clark's since the days of the Book Thieves, while Clark himself served as an associate editor of the volume. Under their guidance a small army of historians, writers, collectors, and librarians were recruited to canvass the state for materials and to write up brief accounts of their findings. Many of these researchers were new members, so to speak, of the press family, being associated with institutions of the press consortium. The editors and Denbo devised the general scheme of the book and, working from the offices of the Press, culled and organized the myriad pieces, pictorial and verbal, gathered by the volunteer contributors. The book with its numerous color illustrations was an unusually elaborate and expensive undertaking for the Press. Clark's contacts in Frankfort proved helpful in securing needed financial support from the state departments of Parks and of Public Information. This support also made possible a very reasonable price, and the first printing of 20,000 copies sold out a few days after its release. *Kentucky: A Pictorial History* reached an audience eager to read about their state and created a store of good will for the consortium and its members.

In 1986, at the age of eighty-three, when most individuals would be well content to take their ease and contemplate whatever achievements they may have enjoyed, Thomas D. Clark became an important contributor to yet another project for his beloved Kentucky. In that year he was appointed by Governor Martha Layne Collins to the Kentucky Bicentennial Commission, which was set up to make plans for commemorating the two hundredth anniversary of Kentucky's statehood in 1992. One of the aims of the Commission was to provide for Kentuckians a better understanding of the history and culture of their homeland. To fill this aim Clark advocated to his fellow Commission members that the Commission sponsor publication of a state encyclopedia. This proposal found ready approval, and Clark secured the services of John E. Kleber, at the time professor of history at Morehead State University, as general editor. Clark and two other historians agreed to be associate editors. A daunting task faced the staff of the encyclopedia-in-the-making, made no less easy by a stringent schedule. Not only had they to establish the criteria for inclusion in the compilation but they also had the painstaking task of outlining possible subjects—who, what, and how much to be included within the practical limits of the proposed volume. And then they had to find writers for the more than 2,000 eventual entries. A professional manuscript editor was included in the staff to review the materials as they were submitted and to prepare them for publication, and a close liaison was established with the Press to ease the actual production of the volume.

Clark was on hand at every step of this demanding process, ready with his counsel matured through years of research, writing, and publishing and grounded on the foundation of his seemingly inexhaustible knowledge of all things Kentucky. He himself contributed nearly one hundred entries and somehow found the time to review the entire manuscript before it went to the printer. Through his unstinting efforts—and those of all the others who participated in creating the volume—*The Kentucky Encyclopedia* was published on schedule in June 1992 to wide praise. Though it lacked the visual appeal of the much earlier *Pictorial History*, it quickly became one of the most widely distributed titles ever issued by the University Press of Kentucky. Thanks to Thomas D. Clark's foresight and dedication, the *Encyclopedia* remains a fitting and enduring commemoration of the commonwealth's entry into the union of states.

Clark's involvement with the publishing world is, of course, by no means limited to the Kentucky press. As a widely published author he came to know such notable American publishers as John Farrar of Farrar & Rinehart and Alfred A. Knopf. On the academic side he was likewise closely acquainted with three pioneering directors of southern university presses—William Couch of the University of North Carolina Press, Marcus Wilkerson of the Louisiana State University Press, and Savoie Lottinville of the University of Oklahoma Press. Nearer home, he has from time to time encouraged and advised local private publishers. One of these is the Henry Clay Press of Lexington, which issues items of local interest—a collection of newspaper articles by Clark's friend J. Winston Coleman and a reprint of Clark's own *The Kentucky* among other titles. Another such publisher is the Jesse Stuart Foundation, which specializes in books about Kentucky and the Appalachian region with a focus on providing materials for use in schools. One of their titles is a reissue of Clark's book for children, *Simon Kenton: Frontiersman.*

In addition to his long involvement with the writing and publishing of books, Clark was also involved at a crucial time in the editing and management of the *Journal of Southern History.* The journal was first issued in 1935. It was the voice of the recently formed Southern Historical Association, which had grown out of the new sense of professionalism among historians in the South. First based at Louisiana State University, the journal, along with the *Southern Review,* fell victim to a financial scandal in the university administration. It was then taken up by Vanderbilt University. In the late 1940s, for reasons that are not entirely clear, the Vanderbilt administration decided to end its sponsorship. Though some other institutions expressed vague interest in the journal, it was Thomas D. Clark and the University of Kentucky that agreed to sustain it. Clark became the managing editor, assisted by Merton England, and in 1949 they brought out their first issue. The two editors had to scramble mightily to find articles and reviews for the first issues as the editorial cupboard was almost bare when they opened it. As universities expanded in the postwar years and as scholars picked up careers interrupted by the war, the task of finding submissions became easier. At one point the editors expressed the complaint, doubtless common to editors everywhere, of reviewers who continually exceeded their prescribed allotments of space. In 1952 Clark went to India to lecture for the State Department, and Merton England succeeded him as managing editor of the journal. Five years later England announced his resignation, and shortly afterward the university, in a manner reminiscent of Vanderbilt, reported that it would no longer sponsor the journal. Fortunately Rice Institute stepped forward to provide a new home. Clark felt that his intervention had saved the journal when it appeared that no other institution would take it. Sometime later he was largely responsible for the creation of an index to the *Journal of Southern History* as well as of one for the *Journal of American History*, enduring legacies of his involvement.

Truly it can be said of Thomas D. Clark that in the beginning was the word and that word was history, animate and animating, a vital thing that could enliven all who would harken to its voice. During a long and productive life he has preached this word—through his many books and other publications, in the lecture hall to thousands of students, in talks before assemblies large and small. In less direct ways he has made manifest not just the word of history but of much else besides in his fostering of the publication of books and articles. This fostering was perhaps best realized in his involvement with the University Press of Kentucky. Though he disclaims any credit for being the father of the Press, it cannot be denied that he was behind it at every step—arguing, cajoling, and demanding—until it came to fruition. Without him there might well have been no fruition at all. While every book issued by the Press bears its imprint for all to see, it also carries, unseen but nonetheless present, the name of Thomas D. Clark. Imprimatur.

NOTES

I could not have written this essay without the assistance of many individuals. I would like to mention especially Kenneth W. Elliott, former assistant director of the University Press of Kentucky, who shared his recollections with me, and Thomas D. Clark, who with his customary generosity, talked with me at length about his experiences. My thanks to everyone who contributed throughts and materials. What I have done with them is, of course, on my head.

1. Author interview with Thomas D. Clark, Oct. 8, 2002.

PART IV. THE FRIEND

Colleague

Mary Wilma Hargreaves

I first met Thomas D. Clark at a faculty reception on the lawn at Maxwell Place on a fall evening in 1948. He was then head of the history department at the University of Kentucky, while I was a mere doctoral candidate at Radcliffe immersed in writing a dissertation about settlement in the American West. Since I was working under an exponent of the thesis of Frederick Jackson Turner—that American democracy was an outgrowth of the development of successive frontiers on cheap public land, a view widely discussed among historians of that period—I raised the topic in our conversation. Clark replied that his own approach was directed to the social and economic background of the settlement, with no attention to its political history. He proposed a far broader palette than the interpretively deterministic implications of the closing frontier.

I again met him the following spring when he invited me to lecture on American land policy before one of his classes while he was to be out of town. Since the topic was basic to my research, I readily agreed. It was my first teaching assignment, and I appreciated the experience. Two years later, with degree in hand, I applied for permanent employment in his department. Ultimately, when history classes had swelled beyond the walls of Frazee Hall to the auditorium of Memorial Hall, I was placed on the tenure track of teaching, but for some thirteen years my collegial role was that of research editor.

In assuming leadership of the history department in the fall of 1942, Clark had adopted the goal of making it one of the outstanding departments in the field. Through the war years that was a staggering ambition. Several faculty members who had been on military leave returned by 1946, but there were then only nine on the staff. Courses were limited to two broad fields, the history of the United States and that of Europe, although in the university catalogue they were broken down into twenty-two courses dealing with the various nations at varying time periods. A course was then listed also for colonial Latin America and the Latin American republics, but eight years later Clark's departmental report spoke of "Latin America lying at our very door . . . all but a void on this campus." At that time, too, he noted that "just this year" had it been possible "to deal with Canada as a separate part of the British Empire." The report for 1954 also called for "a dependable scholar" who could cover "that great historical and geographic void, Russia," and the same for China, as well as an "orientalist" to teach the history of the Near and Far East.[1] By the mid-1960s, when Clark resigned as head of the department, the number of catalogued courses had been increased to sixty-six, plus three seminars. The number of faculty members had grown to twenty. Clark believed that there had been "remarkable headway in accomplishing a subject area balance in . . . course offerings," but warned against "premature pressures to enter areas where we are neither equipped by library holdings, nor pressed by student demands."[2]

Expansion of the variety of courses and the size of the faculty was only one aspect of the approach to developing departmental standing. Clark's "town and gown" relationships had brought him into close friendship with a group of local history enthusiasts, among them Judge Samuel M. Wilson, one of the original members of the Henry Clay Foundation, to which body Mrs. Thomas Bullock, great-granddaughter of Henry Clay, in 1948 bequeathed her home, Ashland, the

Henry Clay Estate, and its furnishings. This included numerous letters of the Kentucky statesman, most of which were unpublished. In 1952 Clark, himself one of the early members of the Foundation, entered into a collaborative project for the University of Kentucky history department and the University of Kentucky Press to collect, edit, and publish as complete as possible a compilation of the Henry Clay papers.

The project was sponsored as part of a program by the National Archives and Records Division of the federal government and, beginning in 1957, was funded by a grant from the Eli Lilly Endowment. When that grant was later exhausted, federal appropriations through the General Services Administration continued the financing. The Clay Papers Project was only the second in a series that over time has been extended to publication of the correspondence of a large array of public figures. Its development came at a stage to establish precedents as standards of editorial style and criteria for the broad program; and the Clay volumes, ultimately totaling eleven, were highly acclaimed by reviewers.

The program also provided for acquisition of a massive collection of documentary material for scholarly research, not only by local faculty and students but also by visiting scholars, some even from abroad. The National Archives supplied microfilm copies of the extensive holdings of Clay Papers in the Library of Congress and the State Department archival files. The local staff searched for and obtained microfilm copies of documents wherever else they could be found. Dr. James F. Hopkins of the UK history department, long an associate of Clark in shared Mississippi background and academic roots, was appointed editor-in-chief; I was employed as the associate editor. Over the years the National Archives assigned several fellowship trainees as assistants who subsequently assumed editorial roles on similar projects at other universities.

The Clay Project was a giant step in promoting the academic standing of the history department. Publication of the *Journal of Southern History*, organ of the Southern Historical Association, by faculty members from editorial headquarters in the UK history department made a similar contribution over the period 1948-59. Participation by departmental personnel in professional organizations of the discipline was also effective. Attendance at sessions of the Southern Historical Association was virtually mandatory. Various members of the faculty were active on its committees; one was secretary-treasurer for many years and Clark, a life member, was president of the body in 1947. He was also president of the Mississippi Valley Historical Association in 1957 and chairman of the executive committee for the next six years, at the end of which the organization changed its name and the scope of its program to a broader basis as the Organization of American Historians. Clark was executive secretary of the latter body from 1970 to 1973.

His role in resurrecting the UK chapter of the honorary history fraternity, Phi Alpha Theta, served further to enhance the distinction of the department. Tau Chapter had been very active prior to World War II and had hosted the national convention of the organization in 1939. It had, however, become "a wartime casualty," as officers of the parent body lamented. In 1946 it remained the only chapter that had not been reactivated.

Despite repeated urging by the national secretary, reorganization languished. Clark's response to inquiries was that such a matter required student initiative. Finally in 1951, when the national organization proposed holding a banquet in conjunction with the annual meeting of the Mississippi Valley Historical Association in Cincinnati, Clark agreed to serve as speaker and invited the national secretary to come to Lexington for reactivation of the local chapter. Clark served as toastmaster for similar banquets of the national body held in conjunction with meetings of the Mississippi Valley Historical Association the following two years, and in the latter year the sessions were held in Lexington. His activity with the national organization of Phi Alpha Theta subsequently continued, and from 1957 through 1959 he served as its president.

Meanwhile Tau Chapter blossomed. Members prepared papers for presentation at regional meetings, and on one occasion the chapter was designated as regional leader for its performance. The annual chapter banquet, held in conjunction with initiation of the department's honor students, became annually the occasion for announcement of faculty book awards, distinguished professorships, and similar honors.

That the contacts Clark developed through his professional activities resounded in recognition for the department was evidenced in his ability to find notable and interesting speakers for community as well as academic audiences. From 1949 until his retirement he was chairman of a university committee to present the Blazer Lecture Series. That program was the outgrowth of a friendship that had developed between Clark and Paul Blazer, president of the Ashland Oil Company, during lengthy efforts to raise public interest in state constitutional reform. The movement having failed, Blazer asked Clark what could be done to awaken community interest in civic affairs. Clark suggested a lecture program, and as a Christmas gesture Mr. and Mrs. Blazer funded through the university an annual series known as the Blazer Lectures in History and Social Sciences, free and open to the public.

Initially six talks were given each year, sometimes with an additional one in the summer months. They presented nationally distinguished leaders in a broad range of fields—history, economics, political science, sociology, philosophy, theology, law, and education. They were college professors and presidents, governmental representatives, and popular social commentators such as Vance Packard. Primarily, however, they were historians, the leading scholars in the field, specialists on a wide range of subjects—diplomatic and military, the Constitution and international law, American and European, even South African in that era of apartheid tension. Occasionally the lectures paralleled a series coordinated with and sponsored by the English department; sometimes they were incorporated with state education conferences and other scholarly meetings. A flyer advertising the agenda for 1962 commented that over the past twelve years the Blazer Lectures had discussed many fields of interest relating to the status of individuals in a society "overwhelmingly urban and industrial," requiring "marked reappraisal of human values." For students who read in classes publications by authors they could now hear "live," the experience held special interest. The intellectual climate of the university was notably elevated.

With Clark's retirement as head of the history department, administration of the program was shifted to the more broadly based administration of the College of Arts and Sciences. Funding was reduced and the number of lectures diminished. Although the lectures were continued into the 1990s, they numbered only one or two a year. The leadership that had given them focus was no longer evident.

Elsewhere in this volume Clark's roles as educator and inspirer are discussed. As early as 1934 he had begun to establish ties as a visiting professor. For periods of varying length he held that status at numerous universities—Rochester, North Carolina, Chicago, Claremont, Harvard, Wyoming, Penn State, Western Tennessee Teachers' College, Wisconsin, Kent State, Stanford, and the University of Washington, with longer appointments at the universities of Tennessee, Indiana, Louisville, and Eastern Kentucky.

These were years when administrators at the University of Kentucky were placing strong emphasis upon the importance of foreign travel as a cultural influence. Globalization had not yet become a cliché, but faculty members were urged to go abroad, particularly if they were teaching courses relating to foreign lands. One who taught European history was expected to travel the areas he would be discussing. Kentuckians, it was argued, were far too isolated, too insular in their appreciation of other societies. Clark's travel itinerary reflected the trend and further extended his range of connections.

During the summer of 1948 he participated in the Salzburg Seminar in Austria, and two years later he returned to Austria as a "visiting expert" for an American history program conducted by the United States army. In 1952 he lectured during a three-month tour of India. The next year he delivered a summer lecture series at Oxford University. For five months during the winter of 1961-62 he served under NATO auspices as a professor at universities in Athens and Thessaloniki, Greece. In June 1965 he addressed a joint American-Yugoslavian seminar at Novi Sad. For Clark, at least, these excursions proved the worth of the emphasis on travel abroad. From Greece he wrote to colleagues back home of the "tremendously stimulating experience." He concluded: "I feel that I have learned a lot, seen a lot, and been confused a lot by what I have seen."[3]

Such activities were not, however, without personal strain. When the Clay Project began operations, we inherited office space that had once been the quarters of the librarian Margaret I. King, and I inherited her desk. In it I found a glass and an empty milk carton. I was somewhat puzzled that these artifacts remained so long after Miss King's departure. Dr. Hopkins provided the explanation. Clark had been using the space as a library study, and he had a peptic ulcer. The affliction grew worse under stress. The "medical advice" that had finally compelled him to decline the invitation to address the banquet of the national organization of Phi Alpha Theta at Cincinnati in 1951 stemmed from a mandate that he abjure "over-activity." He suffered acutely while writing *Frontier America*, one of his major works, pub-

· lished in 1958. Eventually he underwent major surgery to alleviate the problem, but while teaching at Indiana University in 1966 he wrote to a Lexington colleague that a bout of flu had "touched off" his ulcer, and he expressed resignation that he would carry it through life. "You don't know how much I have suffered from it," he commented.[4]

Clark's interest in timberland development probably alleviated the pressure. He and Hopkins purchased some tracts of forestland in the hills of Estill County in the early 1950s and began frequent Saturday excursions in an old Jeep, reviewing their holdings, getting acquainted with their new neighbors, and "traveling the back roads of Kentucky." They hired local labor to harvest their mature timber and reforested it with pine seedlings. Years later Clark wrote to "Hop" from Europe of his regret that they no longer continued their Saturday walks in the woods.

In 1957, however, Clark found an alternative: summers when he was not traveling he would spend in South Carolina. There had been a fire in Frazee Hall and that summer the building was under reconstruction. Perhaps his married daughter's residence in Columbia, South Carolina, provided further attraction. The Clarks acquired a tree farm named Turnbull Plantation, near Blair. Clark found life there "wonderfully free of interruptions."[5] He could then make good progress in his writing. Office hubbub in Lexington made such achievement difficult. He sometimes alluded to hours of nighttime electricity burning as he worked at home. I found him once during the comparative quiet of the lunch hour pecking away at a manuscript on an old Underwood typewriter. Freedom from interruption gave special value to the summers in South Carolina. The "progress" to which he had alluded was evidenced as he later informed his secretary that he was sending two chapters to be typed and the following day added a third.

Tom's persistence in research and writing rested upon his belief that good teaching required it. Researchers, he contended, have a breadth of vision lacking in those not so engaged. Some kind of "creative production" was "almost a necessity" for the scholar if he was "to keep his mind active, his teaching forceful, and his personal outlook wholesome."[6] Prior to his retirement he himself wrote fifteen works, coauthored one, and edited three, several of them multivolumed. Since then his bibliography has grown by at least nineteen titles as author, eleven as coauthor, four as editor, and eleven as author of an introduction.

While he denied that the history department operated under a "publish or perish" regimen, Clark offered "strong encouragement" for such productivity. He had insisted, as he began his administration, that appointments to the history faculty be made through his office, not by the dean. The action not only stabilized his authority but also enabled him to plan development of subject areas in the course structure and to adjust teaching loads as seemed appropriate for individual capabilities. A faculty member who required summer leave to pursue research away from campus or one who had need for uninterrupted time to complete a manuscript found a sympathetic response. He deplored the plethora of committee assignments with which university officials burdened the faculty complaining that the duties had more to do with administration than scholarship. Under his leadership administrative assignments and heavier teaching duties tended to fall to the lot of staff members unproductive in publication.

Notwithstanding the scope of his academic endeavors, Clark was a meticulous administrator. On one occasion he sent out a general memorandum to his colleagues reminding them that as director of graduate studies he was supposed to sign every graduate thesis and that he expected not only to see the cover pages but "to look it through carefully before signing."[7] Sometimes he called upon various members of the staff to carry on routine administrative duties during his absence. On one such occasion, when a schedule for the following year would be required, he left a memorandum of the factors to be considered: "there are so many," he explained. "We have to think of the load, the quality of the program, the coverage, trying to take care of productive men, the graduate program. All these things have to be weighed carefully."[8] When the proposed arrangements were later submitted to him for review, he considerably revised them.

Subsequently a departmental secretary, serving also as Clark's personal secretary, assumed many of the routine responsibilities. During his absences she kept the postal service active transmitting queries and keeping him informed. When stenographic duties for faculty as well as Tom finally became overwhelming, a typist was added to the staff.

Clark once alluded to the "family-like" atmosphere of the history department. The staff at that time was still relatively small, and it was close-knit in its relationships. Members knew one another's family ties and concerns. Births were congratulated; illnesses, even of relatives beyond the immediate family, were sympathetically recognized. There was considerable consultation and flexibility in course assignment and scheduling. But family tensions do arise, and occasionally they developed in our midst. Clark held monthly faculty meetings at which members were sometimes asked to read papers. The subsequent critiques occasionally grew heated. Clark remembers one over slavery; I, myself, drew fire when I mentioned the Democratic-Republican Party of Henry Clay's affiliation during the late 1790s. One of our more conservative brothers objected to such a hyphenated organization. As he filed his last report on the department, Clark noted that he had steadily strived to maintain *esprit de corps*.

His role as *pater familias* also included long, persistent effort to improve the teaching environment. His annual reports to the dean regularly pointed to the need for better facilities. His concern for expanded library and archival holdings is discussed elsewhere in this volume. He believed that such development attracted better faculty. As new fields were added to the curriculum, the department's requests for library materials increased from a couple of hundred dollars a year in the 1940s to approximately $15,000 by 1963, without including additions to reference works, periodicals, and the documentary collection. He was pleased when the library holdings had grown to a million volumes but he deplored the closing of the library early in the evening, the difficulty of finding catalogued materials that turned out to be "missing," and the lack of cubicles available to graduate students. He also worked to promote development of the University Press as an outlet for faculty publication and took pride in its numerous volumes that represented work of the history faculty.

His most vigorous criticism centered on the limited space that made it necessary that faculty share offices. He was insistent that there be privacy for student consultation and quiet for reading and reflection to support lecture preparation. He found it "damnable" that seminars had to be held in large classrooms and similarly objectionable that the number of classrooms available for the history department had been reduced from the nine to which it had had access in 1929 to only five in 1965, when the number of students had increased eightfold. He also lamented the crowding of secretarial staff and saw no way to improve the situation but to "butcher" his own office "and to destroy the already limited privacy."[9] He even sought an elevator so that "elderly professors" could more easily reach Frazee Hall's third-floor classrooms.

Some of the desired structural improvement was effected when Frazee Hall was reconstructed in 1957. A seminar room and an elevator were provided, but space was still limited. Faculty offices were still shared, and Clark's office was reduced to a cubbyhole, allowing space for little more than a chair, a desk, and a typewriter. Most of his recommendations were incorporated in the construction of the Patterson

Office Tower after he had retired—seminar rooms, private offices, department office suites with separate rooms for the secretary and the chairman—and in the adjoining White Hall classroom building. It seemed as if Clark's protestations had patterned the design.

His annual reports to the dean were frank appraisals of the conditions he deplored and of the progress achieved. His assessment of entering students was one that has been repeated over and over in more recent comment on the state's educational system. He lamented their poor academic preparation, their lack of experience in gathering information and writing papers: "We hear with a monotonous refrain that 'this is the first time I have had to write a paper.'"[10] Students entered and even left the university "oblivious to the wide ramifications of world civilization." Even worse, he contended, "Hundreds of them come and go still in a virginal intellectual state regarding the history of their state and country."[11] A decade later he was beginning to see students "of much better quality," but he continued to find three "serious barriers": they spelled "with difficulty," their ideas were "far more adolescent than they should be at their stage of maturity," and they remained "unwilling, or . . . unable, to read much beyond their textbooks."[12] He did, however, report major improvement by their junior and senior years.

Summing up the accomplishments of the department in the twenty years before his retirement, he reported publication of thirty-two books that had received "critical commendation" in professional journals, at least fifty "sound" articles, and many more of somewhat lesser importance. Few professional meetings had not included one or more papers by members of the department, and others besides Clark had served as officers and committee members of such organizations. Four faculty members had held Guggenheim Fellowships, at least as many had held Fulbright grants, several others had held visiting professorships in the United States or abroad, and one had been named Pitt

Professor at Cambridge, England. Four had been named Distinguished Professor by the UK College of Arts and Sciences, and Clark
himself held permanent rank as Distinguished Professor of the University by vote of the Board of Trustees. Graduate students, too, were
achieving professional distinction. Several were teaching at major universities; two had become state archivists, three others headed university archives, and three held major staff positions at prominent historical societies. Clark had proved a successful entrepreneur in establishing
the history department as one of prominence in the field.

He resigned as head of the department in the spring of 1965,
taught at Indiana University in 1966 and 1967 and at Eastern Kentucky University in the spring of 1967, but returned to the University of Kentucky to teach the spring semester of 1968. He retired there
the following July.

As he reviewed the progress and looked to the future of the department, Clark warned of developing problems. His lengthy administration had been marked by remarkable continuity in the faculty.
Now four members, "the bone sinew of the Department for two decades," would soon be retiring. They would need to be replaced by
"productive scholars—not of the home grown variety"—who would
be "costly." If the department was to maintain its standing, "some very
realistic adjustments" would need to be made.[13]

Clark had long insisted that senior faculty should teach students
at the entering level. "The most effective teaching a department of
history does in the entire scope of its instructional program," he continued, "is that performed at the freshman and sophomore levels."[14]
But in recent years the department had been confronted with greatly
increasing numbers of incoming students while at the same time it
was giving much time and mature scholarship to staffing the graduate program. In the school year 1961-62 the course schedule had been
revised "to offer larger sections with superior lecturers and as gener-

ous use of . . . graduate assistants as possible to help conduct classes more economically as to time and cost."[15] The dilemma now posed required funding to replace senior faculty for maintenance of a rigorous graduate program while coping with the pressure of the increasing student load at the vital entering levels.

"I can only hope," he concluded, "that as the university grows in size of staff and numbers of the student body a genuine effort will be made to maintain some degree of personal relationship between the staff and the student."[16]

NOTES

1. University of Kentucky History Department, *Annual Report,* 1953-54, 7.
2. UK History Dept., *Annual Report,* 1964-65, 4.
3. Thomas D. Clark to Neva Armstrong, Dec. 27, 1961.
4. Thomas D. Clark to Robert Lunde, March 4, 1966.
5. Thomas D. Clark to Rhea Taylor, July 27, 1957.
6. UK History Dept., *Annual Report,* 1963, 3.
7. Thomas D. Clark to Staff, June 20, 1958.
8. Thomas D. Clark to Rhea Taylor, July 27, 1961.
9. UK History Dept., *Annual Report,* 1953-54, 10; 1963, 7; 1965, 10.
10. UK History Dept., *Annual Report,* March 1955, 1.
11. UK History Dept., *Annual Report,* 1953-54, 7.
12. UK History Dept., *Annual Report,* 1963, 1-2.
13. UK History Dept., *Annual Report,* 1964-65, 7-8.
14. Ibid., 6.
15. UK History Dept., *Annual Report,* 1961, 7.
16. UK History Dept., *Annual Report,* 1964-65, 6.

Southern Writer

WADE HALL

When I moved to Louisville in late December of 1962, I already knew that Kentucky was the home of Daniel Boone, Mrs. Wiggs, the Little Colonel, Jesse Stuart, and Thomas D. Clark. I had met Boone in a history class and Mrs. Wiggs, the Little Colonel, and Stuart in my English classes. Moreover, Stuart was a real person still alive and had saved my career when I was a discouraged, nineteen-year-old first-year teacher in a small town in South Alabama. One afternoon after classes the school librarian saw me sitting disconsolately in the reading room and asked me my problem. "Oh, nothing," I said. "I've just decided that I'm a failure as a teacher." She said, "Honey, you are too young to be a failure at anything. Wait a minute. I have something to cheer you up." When she returned, she handed me a copy of Jesse Stuart's *The Thread That Runs So True* and said, "Take this book home tonight and read it. I guarantee you'll feel a lot better tomorrow."

Indeed, I did. Jesse Stuart's autobiographical account of an Eastern Kentucky schoolteacher's travails and triumphs inspired me to regroup my resources and attack the challenges of my restless thirteen- and fourteen-year-olds with renewed vigor. I finished my first year of teaching successfully, fled the schoolhouse, and spent two years in the U.S. Army, completed two graduate degrees, and was teaching at the University of Florida when I finally met Stuart in person. He had been invited to speak to our students, and the head of the English

159

department asked me to drive from Gainesville over to the Jacksonville airport to pick him up. By the time we arrived at the university we had bonded completely, and he was calling me Wade and insisting that I call him Jesse. Within a year I had accepted an appointment to the faculty of Kentucky Southern College, a bold new school being built in Louisville. The experimental college lasted only nine years, but my friendship with Jesse Stuart lasted until his death in 1984. My friendship with Kentucky and Kentuckians has lasted longer.

I had met Thomas D. Clark earlier, in the closed stacks of the Rare Book Room (now Special Collections) at the University of Illinois in Urbana, where I had gone to study for a Ph.D. in English. I already knew Clark's name and had used his books, though sparingly, in writing undergraduate and graduate papers at Troy State University and the University of Alabama, but it was at Illinois that I got to know him in depth. I soon realized that for him, as for many southerners, history was a natural vocational choice. He had been born and had grown up in Mississippi, a state where, in the words of William Faulkner, the past wasn't even past. For many southerners, it was also a burden, a challenge, an obstacle—a puzzling gift to be opened, examined, and understood. As a youngster I had been bitten by the history bug and had double-majored in English and history at Troy State in my home state of Alabama. Later, I took a master's degree in English at the University of Alabama, where, in addition to such required courses as Anglo-Saxon and philology, I concentrated in American literature. My service in the army had taken me away from the Southland for the first time and given me a new perspective and a useful aesthetic distance from my own history and culture, while sharpening my interest in them.

After I finished the course work, my adviser at Illinois, John T. Flanagan, suggested that I use the university's recently acquired Franklin J. Meine Collection of American Humor and Folklore in choosing and researching my subject. On a visit with Professor Flanagan to examine the collection in the closed stacks, I noticed a number of books by Clark as well as numerous other books by southerners about the South. I said, "Y'all have a lot of books about my part of the country. I wonder if I could find a dissertation topic in them." Professor Flanagan said, "Wade, you can easily find a dozen topics about the South in this collection. You could do most of your research in these stacks." I accepted his challenge to write about the South, secured a permanent pass to the restricted stack area, and set about discovering a topic.

Nine months and a couple of letters later, I had my dissertation finished, with the bulk of the research having been done in the Meine Collection, augmented by occasional forays into the university's huge main library as well as several days of field research in the files of my hometown newspaper, *The Union Springs* (Alabama) *Herald*. Even though I was teaching English full-time, I managed to have a completed copy of my study waiting for Professor Flanagan when he returned to Illinois from a Fulbright Lectureship in Belgium and Germany. I had hired a secretary at the university to type a clean copy, which I photocopied for the members of my dissertation committee. It ran over eight hundred pages and was bound in two volumes. When I took a copy to Arthur Scott, the American history professor on my committee, and handed him volume one, he said, "Goodness, you Southerners do write long dissertations." I said brashly, "Yes, I suppose we do, and here is the second volume. We have a lot to say."

I don't know if all five members of my committee read every word of both volumes; but after I had defended it and was excused from the room while they discussed my performance, one of them came to the door and said, "Congratulations, Mr. Hall, we think you've written a fine book." Needless to say, I was elated by their response and began to think that maybe I could find a publisher who would agree with them. After I had accepted a position as an assistant professor of English at the University of Florida, I decided to see if the University Press on campus agreed that I had written a book. *Mirabile dictu!* They did. In fact, within a few months the Press had published a monograph for me in their humanities series, entitled *Reflections of the Civil War in Southern Humor.* In 1965, almost three years after I had moved to Kentucky, I received my first copy of the entire study, *The Smiling Phoenix: Southern Humor, 1865-1914.* I was utterly spoiled by my good fortune in having my dissertation yield two publications, a monograph and a book. The book was widely reviewed, mostly favorably, including a positive notice in *The New York Times Book Review.* Both the monograph and the book sold out soon after publication, and the book was reprinted. I would never again be able to duplicate that success.

My heavy teaching and administrative load at Kentucky Southern College, and later at Bellarmine College, put a damper on some of my scholarly ambitions. Fortunately, I met Thomas D. Clark in person soon after I arrived in Kentucky. We quickly became friends and he became an inspiration and a role model for me. Not only was he a productive scholar but he also taught a full load of courses, chaired the Department of History at the University of Kentucky, mentored numerous graduate students, and made speeches from one end of Kentucky to the other, sometimes spilling over into other states. Moreover, for four years he edited the *Journal of Southern History* and was active in several professional organizations for historians. He set a high standard for the scholar-professor such as I aspired to be.

While writing my dissertation at Illinois (my subject, how humor reflected and sustained the South, could easily have served for a degree in history) I got to know numerous books by the great historians of the South, past and present, from Francis Butler Simpkins and

C. Vann Woodward to Wilbur J. Cash, Ulrich B. Phillips, and Howard Odum. None of them was more useful or meaningful to me than Thomas D. Clark. His books held up the clearest mirror to the South that I knew. Of at least a dozen books by Clark that I consulted, four were especially useful sources for my research: *The Rampaging Frontier* (1939); *Pills, Petticoats, and Plows: The Southern Country Store* (1944); *The Rural Press and the New South* (1948); and *The Southern Country Editor* (1948).

I was impressed not only by the number and cogency of his books but also by the fact that, like me, he was from the Deep South—or Lower South, as he likes to say—and could write affectionately, critically, and eloquently about our native region. Here was a man I could emulate, a model for my own youthful ambitions to, in the words of his fellow Mississippian, William Faulkner (whom he knew), "tell about the South." In *Absalom, Absalom!*, one of the twentieth century's great novels about the nineteenth century, Faulkner tells his fictional story about the South when he sends Quentin Compson to Harvard, where he has a Canadian roommate named Shreve McCannon who becomes intrigued about Quentin's land of violence and gentility. He wants Quentin to explain to him his mysterious homeland south of the Ohio River and asks these provocative questions: "What's it like there? What do they do there? Why do they live there? Why do they live at all?" And Quentin, who is Faulkner's mouthpiece, responds, "You can't understand it. You would have to be born there." Nevertheless, he tries to explain the South to Shreve by telling him a story, the archetypal story of a poor Virginia mountain boy named Thomas Sutpen who moves to Mississippi and brutally carves out a fiefdom for himself on the backs of slaves and poor whites. No one has told the story of the American South any better or more accurately in fiction than William Faulkner, and to my knowledge, no one has written better nonfiction about the South than Thomas D. Clark.

When I was reading his books in the Illinois library, I did not know Clark personally, but I could tell from their contents that we had a lot in common. Biographical sources provided additional evidence of our kinship. We were both born near the 33rd parallel, he in Louisville, Winston County, Mississippi, on June 14, 1903, and I near Union Springs in Bullock County, Alabama, some thirty-one years later. His community in east central Mississippi was hardly forty miles, as the crow flies, from the Alabama border. In addition to the African Americans descended from slaves who made up a majority of the population in both our counties, we both grew up in a society where most of the whites were descended from English, Scottish, and Scot-Irish immigrants who had settled originally in the Carolinas and Virginia before the American Revolution.

Despite our age difference, our boyhood experiences were similar. My community was even more of a cultural backwater than Clark's and had changed very little from my grandparents' time to my own. As sons of the rural South, therefore, Clark and I shared the same church (Baptist) and politics (Democratic). Such regional fixtures as the country store, the rural newspaper, the country school, the family-worked farm, and the passenger train that he describes so accurately in his books were the reality of my boyhood. Except for motorized transportation, we had hardly any of the conveniences of twentieth-century life. When I was a young boy we had no electricity, telephones, running water, or indoor plumbing. I was aware, of course, that such marvels existed as close as Union Springs and a bit farther away, in Montgomery, where we made occasional trips for legal, business, and medical reasons. I also saw movie versions of modern life at the Lilfred Theater in Union Springs, where we saw picture shows once or twice a year. When I used a telephone for the first time as a freshman in college, I knew, therefore, that you picked up the receiver and said "hello"—a word that we country people never used—

into one end and listened at the other end. I also practiced movie-learned etiquette the first time I ever ate in a restaurant as a college senior.

In the Lower South, it was not uncommon for families to nickname their sons, often with their initials, and I remember men who went through life known only as H.T. (he had a son called T.C.) or J.T. or V.L. or J.W. or Q.P., who was a deacon in our church. When I was an infant, so she told me, my mother decreed that none of her children would be tagged with a nickname, but little Tom Clark's mother had no such aversion. She called him T.D. At least, T. D. luckily avoided the nickname that has stuck to one of my cousins all his life: Sweet Thing.

During my boyhood, my family and everyone else in our rural community were still living about the same way my ancestors in Alabama and Clark's in Mississippi had lived in the nineteenth century. In fact, my community was a veritable folk museum that progress had hardly touched since my ancestors had settled in Southeast Alabama before the Civil War. His part of Mississippi had been Choctaw Indian country. Mine had been home to the Creek Indians until General Andrew Jackson moved them to the Oklahoma country, thus clearing the last large Indian territory in Alabama for white settlement.

In my youth, farming was still back-breaking labor that aged and crippled poor whites and blacks alike into an early grave. Both Clark and I grew up close to the cotton fields and knew the backbreaking drudgery of cotton production. Like everyone else, we raised almost all the food we ate in our garden, our fields, and our pastures; and we canned and preserved food for the winter months. We ground our dried corn into meal on a primitive gristmill. We even made our own soap, using fat from our slaughtered hogs and lye water rendered from fireplace ashes. We made our own syrup from the sugar cane we grew, and we slept under quilts made by our womenfolk. My country was a landscape of cotton fields and cotton gins, Fourth of July barbecues, protracted church revivals in the summer, moonshining in the thick woods, and wagons loaded with freshly cut stove wood for the kitchen and house wood to be burned in the fireplaces during the winter.

If Thomas D. Clark had visited my home county or its seat in 1940 or 1950, when I was a boy, he would surely have felt at home. Bullock County and Union Springs were but Alabama versions of his own Winston County and its seat of local government at Louisville. He would have driven through thousands of acres of cotton, peanuts, and corn, still cultivated by mules and field labor, past unpainted tenant shacks without indoor plumbing or electricity, and one-room schoolhouses that grossly underserved rural children, especially African Americans, who, unlike white students riding buses, had to walk to school. Two of my father's sisters lived with their families in log cabins that were smaller versions of the double log house in which Clark was born. Like him, I attended all-white public schools from the first grade through college and remember the dreaded tests for tapeworms that, untreated, weakened and sometimes killed children who were poorly clothed, poorly fed, and poorly doctored.

Clark grew up in the shadow of the Civil War, with Confederate veterans still talking battles and strategies and what-might-have-beens. I grew up in the shadow of Confederate monuments and antebellum attitudes. On Saturdays in my county he would have passed throngs of country people, mostly black, on their way to town by foot, buggy, wagon, car, or truck. In town, he would have driven by the statue of a Confederate soldier at parade rest in front of the courthouse with "Our Heroes" inscribed on its base, and watched the black crowds spill over the sidewalks into the stores and streets. He would have seen numerous "White" and "Colored" signs marking water fountains and entrances to the offices of doctors and dentists and to the Lilfred Theater, where blacks sat in the balcony, sometimes called The Crow's Nest. If he had checked with the county clerk, he would have found that only one black was registered to vote, the black undertaker, and he cast the only Republican vote in the county.

Although we both attended strictly segregated schools and churches, whites and blacks shared lives of unrelenting labor and formed a camaraderie of poor workers in the cotton fields. Bending over to chop weeds from cotton plants in early spring and later to pull the cotton from the tough, piercing bolls in the fall, I dreamed of an escape from a life of such grinding labor. For people like me from families with no money or power or connections, the only escape was through education. At least Clark had a role model in his mother, who was a schoolteacher. I had none except for my teachers at the local country school. Not only was I the first in my family to attend college but I was also the first to graduate from high school. My mother dropped out of school at fifteen when she was in the eighth grade to get married. My father came from a family in which no one was functionally literate. He could write his name crudely and keep simple accounts in his country store, but he could not read a book or newspaper or a document. When he needed something read, my mother read to him.

Clark and I are surely no doppelgangers, but in many ways the journeys of our lives and careers have been parallel. We both have witnessed things that have radically changed the South of our boyhoods: rural electricity, indoor plumbing, and improved roads; the change from segregated, one-room schools to integrated, consolidated schools; the transition from a self-sufficient, agrarian culture to an urban, consumer culture; and the shift from farming to a service-industrial economy. We have seen the decline of the lively businesses on main street in small towns and their replacement by a Wal-Mart commerce. On the other hand, we have seen remarkable advances in medical and dental care and greater access to the arts. In little more than a single generation, our people went from the horse-and-buggy era to the computer and space age—from a predominantly illiterate, oral society to one that is producing college professors, physicians, entrepreneurs, accountants, and lawyers. As I remind my four brothers, who never left our home community, and their families, "In addition to low taxes and clean air, you have all the comforts of city life and none of the hassles."

Truly, the world that Thomas D. Clark and I knew as boys has changed radically. A seismic shift occurred in 1954 when the U. S. Supreme Court outlawed segregation in public schools. The additional aftershocks brought on by civil rights demonstrations and voting and equal-opportunity laws insured that the South would never again be the same. After initial adjustments, progressives in both races admitted that their society was becoming more humane and open to everyone. In particular, life was improving for poor people. Doors were opening onto a true meritocracy. Faulkner chronicles the rise of the rural poor whites in his fictional Yoknapatawpha County in the Snopes Trilogy—*The Hamlet, The Town,* and *The Mansion.* In these novels he follows the rising fortunes of Flem Snopes from son of a tenant farmer and barn burner to prominent businessman in the county seat of Jefferson.

In our own ways and, we hope, with more principles and a higher morality, Clark and I have also left the cotton patch and gone to town—and beyond. Moreover, our inchoate populism has been nourished and vindicated by these revolutionary events, and our innate egalitarianism has flourished. As students of the past, we have always valued not only the princely and the powerful but also the plain people, the grunts, the biblical "hewers of wood and drawers of water," the people whose names die with them. To his great credit, Clark was one of the first historians to put human faces on the landless, the powerless, the tenant farmer, the country storekeeper, the rural editor. He has always shown us that history is not merely statistics or government documents or military strategy. History is people—people who, like us, have lived, worked, struggled, and died. A vignette from his 1939 *Kentucky: A Guide to the Bluegrass State,* for example, takes a rural Kentucky stereotype and gives him life and worth: "The rustic lolling at the street corners of towns and villages may give every evidence of being lost or out of place; but try to get the better of him in a trade and often he will prove master of the situation." Indeed, Clark's books pay homage to the lives and folkways of ordinary people.

Furthermore, his books show that the past is not the exclusive domain of the professional historian. In making the selections for *Bluegrass Cavalcade*, his 1956 anthology of almost two centuries of Kentucky history and culture, he includes the words of the explorer, the traveler, the journalist, the artist, the musician, the humorist, and the novelist. Nonfiction writers such as John Filson, Gilbert Imlay, Henry Clay, Basil Duke, and John James Audubon are joined by such imaginative writers as James Lane Allen, John Fox Jr., and Elizabeth Madox Roberts in profiling the state. In an eight-page excerpt from Robert's novel of the Kentucky frontier, *The Great Meadow* (1930), he says, "the author packs in a full story of a pioneer woman's approach to Kentucky."

In *The Rampaging Frontier* (1939), which he significantly subtitles *Manners and Humors of Pioneer Days in the South and the Middle West,* he is explicit about the democratic base of history: "Too long the historian has neglected the earthy elements of humanity which went into the making of the West. He has written hundreds of learned essays and pamphlets about them, but seldom has he danced with their gals, or rolled on their camp-meeting floors. He has never drunk with the colonels, drilled with the privates, nor dodged their horses in main street and highway races. All of this to the learned fraternity of historians is frivolous, and above all historians must never be frivolous. Of recent years a few bold ones have dared break away from traditional formality to tell some of the rich yarns which amused another generation." Then he previews the book he has written: "My story is human, and it is buckskin, but if there was ever anything in America that was more buckskin than the frontier and its society it has not yet shown its head. There may be those who will ask: Was there not broadcloth? Yes there was. . . . I have sat lightly on rare antique cherry chairs, decorated with ancient needle point, which were made from patterns of Duncan Phyfe and Chippendale. I know there was broadcloth, but there was more—much more—buckskin." And so the common people find their deserved presence in Clark's books.

In my own writing, I have followed his trail. My first book, *The Smiling Phoenix,* plowed some of the same fields that he covered in his *Rampaging Frontier*, that is, the humor and folk culture of the South in the nineteenth century. In my study I somewhat presumptuously proposed to profile the South with humor, during the time of her "greatest turmoil and change." Some 350 pages later I concluded my portrait of the South rather grandly in these words:

> The South had proved that she could be reborn from ashes like the Phoenix. Sam Watkins [a Confederate veteran] once told an allegory of a rooster named Southern Confederacy killed in an Atlanta cock fight. The owner says a serio-comic farewell to the slain bird, plucks its feathers, fries it, and dips his biscuit in its gravy. Though Watkins ended his story here, his work and the work of other humorists helped to make possible a sequel in which the dead barnyard fowl arises as a beautiful bird of mythology. Indeed, the Southern Phoenix arising from the ashes of Richmond and Atlanta

was more glorious than the one sacrificed on the battlefield at Gettysburg. Southern humorists had helped transform the humble feathers of the rooster into the splendid plumage of the Phoenix.

One of Clark's most readable books is his biography of Simon Kenton, the nearly illiterate Kentucky pioneer whose adventures rival those of Daniel Boone. My own travels into Kentucky history and biography—though not as bold or as successful as Clark's—include a script for the Kentucky History Center on the life of early settler Daniel Trabue and a series of oral biographies on such Kentucky worthies as the teacher and civil rights leader Lyman T. Johnson, the country musicians Pee Wee King and Randy Atcher, the artist-naturalist Harlan Hubbard, and the Alabama-born Kentucky mountain writer James Still. All of these books indicate, I hope, my continuing populism and concern for ordinary people who live successful lives. In 1994 I even made a book out of that most democratic form of written communication, the picture postcard. The University Press of Kentucky named it, appropriately, *Greetings from Kentucky.*

Clark and I share many other vocation-related interests. Although my teaching areas have been principally in literature and rhetoric, I have always valued the study of history at all levels and, like Clark, have a passion for local, regional, and frontier history. My pantheon of great writers includes the likes of Walter Webb, Frederick Jackson Turner, Lowell Harrison, and Thucydides as well as Euripides, Dante, Shakespeare, Faulkner, and Robert Penn Warren.

Like Clark, I learned early on the importance of building a good private library with which to buttress work done away from office or school library. I also became fascinated with the history that lies buried in family letters, diaries, and documents, and I started my own crusade to save them from destruction by collecting and placing them in academic archives. I have never been instrumental in founding a university press, as he has with the University Press of Kentucky, but I have learned the inestimable value of academic presses in publishing scholarly and historical writing.

Now, in the early years of the twenty-first century, I have come almost full circle and look south to reclaim my own roots. In the 1970s I began a series of interviews with mostly elderly people in my home community in Alabama. Each time I visited my family, I taped conversations with people I had known all my life—from my mother, my high school math teacher, and two of my aunts to the pastor of the country church I attended as a boy and a woman who had become a bootlegger to support her family after her husband died. Finally, by the mid-1990s I had shaped nineteen of them into a book-length portrait of the people and the places of Bullock County, Alabama, where I grew up. In the preface I wrote: "This collection of voices from a rural Alabama county is but one attempt to show the value of ordinary people—people who never made a lot of money or wielded much power or made any profound discoveries or controlled any events. They are nonetheless fascinating in their ordinariness— as common as a drop of water from the Conecuh River that flows through the county and as familiar as the camellia that still grows in my mother's back yard. With all things, they share the miracle of existence, of having come into this world and participated briefly in its miracle and mystery. I hope the few people whose voices speak from these pages will serve to represent in some measure the unknown people who live and die on this earth and return to the oblivion from which they came."

By the time I had the book ready for publication, I had also known Clark long enough and well enough to impose on him for a favor. One day at a meeting of some sort in Lexington, I was ready to spring the question. "Dr. Clark," I said, "I've been working for almost twenty years on a book about my people in Alabama. I have taken the interviews I did and shaped them into monologues that, I think, reveal a folk culture that deserves to be preserved. I think you will recognize the people. They may remind you of your own boyhood in Mississippi. They may also remind you of your writings about buckskin history. This is my salute to my own southern buckskin roots. Will you lend your good name and write a few words to introduce the book?" I knew he would.

This is a paragraph from the foreword he wrote for *Conecuh People: Words of Life from the Alabama Black Belt,* which was published in 1999: "Historians of the South in large measure have failed to fill in the human interstices of the region. Always there has existed that large segment of humanity which has been treated as little more than a digital blip in the statistical abstraction of Southern history." These common people, my people, were the forgotten people profiled in Frank L. Owsley's seminal study, *Plain Folk of the Old South,* and they were also Thomas D. Clark's people. I had interviewed them and tried to present them as vital parts of southern history and culture as they told the stories of their lives in their own voices. Indeed, they were his people, too, as he says: "I can vouch first-hand for the authenticity of the spirit of these interviews. In my early life in rural Mississippi I was present in such a social, economic, and geographical setting as a member of a family whose roots were back in 'Old' South Carolina. We lived on and off the land in a comparable social and cultural setting." After reading his thoughtful endorsement of my book, I said to myself, "Who knows? Dr. Clark and I may be cousins." After all, thirty-five years after I moved to Kentucky, I discovered that I had kinfolk here. Why not in Mississippi? A genealogist friend has already told me that Elvis, born in Tupelo, and I probably share the same Gilmore ancestor.

In fact, I have always felt at home in Kentucky. The state and its people have been good to me. When I moved to Kentucky more than forty years ago, I had no problem adjusting to my new home. Even though it was more than four hundred miles north of my birthplace in Alabama, I found the people here as friendly and generous and civilized as my own people. Alabama and Mississippi are side-by-side states and naturally share a lot of history and folkways. So if I could so easily acclimate myself to Kentucky, I suspect that young Tom Clark felt at home soon after he arrived in September of 1928. Moonshining and burgoo, for example, were as much a part of life in sister states to the south as they were in Kentucky. If Tom had as typical a boyhood as I did, he already knew how to put those concoctions together. Soon after I moved to Kentucky I discovered that burgoo is just another name for what we called camp stew or Georgia Hash and served on all the high holy days, including church homecomings, family reunions, Fourth of July celebrations, Thanksgiving, and Christmas. What's more, most men down home considered moonshining as natural and inalienable a right as hunting and clearing a newground.

Perhaps, most important, I think that out of our modest origins, Clark and I have both developed deep-seated populist principles, which the fall of Jim Crowism has allowed to flourish. Although there is still much lingering racism in southern society at all levels—as there is in other parts of the nation—at last the large reservoir of incipient good will between the races in the South is leading us closer to a more peaceful and just society.

Should he return now, of course, to either his or my home county, Clark would find a new world which, despite lingering inequities and persistent economic and racial problems, promises a more just and hopeful future for all its citizens. In Bullock County, blacks and whites work side by side in the offices, stores, and workplaces. The Confederate statue has been carefully removed from in front of the courthouse and placed behind the old, unused Episcopal church. Although most white children attend private schools, the public schools are open to all races. With most of the offices now held by blacks, the county is still struggling to provide adequate services for its people and to create opportunities for young people who want to stay. Recently, on a visit home, I stopped by the bridge over the Conecuh River to talk with an elderly black man fishing at the edge of the river. He said he had just moved back to his boyhood home after spending almost half a century in New York. I asked him why he came back. He smiled. "The fishing is better," he said, as he pulled a good-sized bream from the water. Indeed, the horizon looks bright.

Thomas D. Clark would surely know the importance of good fishing holes in a balanced life. And he would know when to talk and when not to talk when the fish are biting. But he would appreciate any opportunity to exercise the gift he inherited from ancestors who made the spoken word into a fine art. There's hardly any place in Kentucky, or a few other states, where people gather to buy books or to honor those who write them that he has not spoken. He and Jesse Stuart are the only two people I've ever known who could probably cause a traffic jam in Grassy Creek or Bailey's Switch or Fairdealing, Kentucky.

Like me, Clark has never forgotten the storytellers of his youth: the teachers, the preachers, the politicians, the war veterans. Attend one of Clark's popular speeches in Lexington or Louisville or Monkey's Eyebrow in his hundredth year and listen to him talk. Why, he looks and sounds for all the world like one of those wizened Confederate veterans he used to see lolling around the courthouse in Louisville, Mississippi, when he was a boy, spinning stories about war and peace. Clark doesn't need to go home again. He never left. Now in his hundredth year he is still a man who knows the difference—if there be any—between a grape and a scuppernong, a polecat and a skunk, peanuts and goobers and ground peas, and this year's crop of fresh pecans and last year's rancid specimens. He may still refer to his father as Daddy and remember what *guano* means in both Mississippi and Peru. When Clark spoke before the University of Kentucky Alumni Club in Louisville on October 3, 2002, and someone in the audience asked him the recipe for his long life, he listed three ingredients: sweet potatoes, collard greens, and black-eyed peas. It was the perfect recipe for a long and productive life that any native of the Lower South could have given in his sleep.

Whatever else it is, history is the story of what people have done—the good and the bad and especially the familiar. In his recent book *The Landscape of History: How Historians Map the Past*, John Lewis Gaddis, who teaches history at Yale, asserts that "It's part of historical consciousness to learn . . . that there is no 'correct' interpretation of the past." At his great age, Clark is still offering to be our personal guide to the past to allow us to experience with him its graces and disgraces. In his book *The People's House: Governor's Mansions of Kentucky* (2002), he opens the door to the Kentucky governor's mansion and invites us to get to know its residents, from Isaac Shelby to Paul Patton, warts and all. In addition to their political dimensions, he brings the governors and their families to life with anecdotes and sidelights and introduces us to people, high and low, who go about the business of being human and fallible—such as the criminal who walked many miles to present himself at the state penitentiary, located across the street from the governor's house, and was then pardoned by the governor; or the governor's son who was twice convicted of killing a wealthy traveler and sentenced to death, then pardoned by his father. Thomas Dionysius Clark is still bringing the past to the present in color and three dimensions by telling stories.

Perhaps one of Kentucky's finest writers, Elizabeth Madox Roberts, spoke about Clark and me, two outlanders who came to Kentucky and made it our home without, however, relinquishing our native land. In a short story, "On the Mountainside," she tells of a young

man fleeing his mountain homeland who meets an old man returning to his home in the mountains after a long absence. Like a Greek
oracle, he lectures the young man in words that the boy won't understand until he is much older: "The places you knowed when you was
a little short-tail boy won't go outen your head or outen your recollections. . . . You may go far, but mark me as I say it, the places you
knowed when you was a little tad will be the strongest in your remem-
brance. It's true, whoever you are and whatever land you come from.
Your whole insides is made outen what you done first."

In a letter to me dated July 18, 2002, Clark noted that "you and
I have traveled much the same road." Indeed, we have. It was my great
fortune to choose the same state he did in which to spend most of my
life. One of the great pleasures of my forty-plus years in Kentucky has
been the opportunity to get to know him personally and to discover
that a great historian can also be a good man of great courtesy, decency,
and generosity. When I was younger and after I had come to know a
number of very talented Mississippians, I used to say that if I had not
been born in Alabama, I would have considered myself fortunate to
have been born in Mississippi. Now, I should add to that statement: "or
to have moved to Kentucky and gotten to know Dr. Thomas D. Clark,
Kentucky's great American historian, who was born in Mississippi."

As a postscript, I offer a poem I wrote for Dr. Clark's ninety-ninth
birthday. In these lines I tried to blend my own interests in literature
and history with his.

A WISE MAN
for Dr. Thomas D. Clark
on his birthday, July 14, 2002

As all wise men and Methodists know,
Life is reckoned not by years but by works.

Chatterton took his 17 years and retreated to the Middle Ages
Leaving almost nothing but a short life.
Keats and Shelley took a few more hours
And built themselves exquisite mansions.
With less than the Bible allotment,
Shakespeare built an imperishable empire
Of 38 rooms and more,
And Lincoln built a seamless nation.

And you, my good man, have been thrice blessed:
You have wedded longevity
With knowledge and industry
Into a library of human feats and follies,
A collection of exempla and cautionary tales
To show how wise our forefathers were,
Though not as wise as they presumed.

Alas, too late you came into our transient world
To walk among the settlers of Plimouth Plantation
Or to celebrate with the revelers of Ma-re Mount
Or to withdraw with the radical Baptists of Providence.
But you have known our South,
From Jamestown to Gulf Shores,
From the rampaging frontier
To the country store stocked with pills, petticoats,
And plows—not to mention the icebox of Dr. Peppers,
The drum of kerosene,
And the aromatic plugs of Brown Mule Chewing Tobacco.
You have traveled the L. & N. Railroad
From Louisville to Louisville,
With protracted forays into the world beyond,
From Oxford to Bloomington.
Only the Lord knows
How far you've come from Mississippi.

Friend

LEONARD P. CURRY

Certainly I consider Thomas D. Clark to be my friend and hope that he thinks of me as his. I took courses under Professor Clark and he directed a thesis and a dissertation that were earlier versions of my first two books, so it is impossible for me to dismiss my experience of having him as a mentor. Moreover, like many other historians of my generation, I have read a number of his books and cannot wipe from my consciousness his contributions as a scholar, nor forget my awareness of the way in which his work has constituted examples and challenges for my own—that is, his role as a publishing scholar.

It is at least possible, however, to call to the minds of the readers of this volume some of the qualities of this remarkable man that influenced his views, statements, and actions and that have been memorable to those of us who have shared his friendship. In these few comments, therefore, I will speak less about myself as a friend of Clark than of the role of Clark as a friend to many others.

One of the characteristics of Tom Clark known to almost everyone acquainted with him is his commitment to the highest quality in everything with which he is involved. This applies to his own work, the work of his students, and the processes of everything connected with the training of history doctoral students at the University of Kentucky. The requirements for admission to degree candidacy in the Department of History a half-century ago included satisfactory performance on eight-hour written examinations in each of four large fields of history, e.g., U. S. history to 1865; U. S. history after 1865; European history after 1789; all of English history, a four-hour written examination in an outside field, and a four-hour oral examination, nominally in the student's major field. All of this was to be completed within one month. In addition Clark's students—and eventually *only* his students—were required to complete within the same period the dreaded "lectures." These were written classroom lectures (i.e., essays) on assigned topics, with instructors' and students' bibliographies, completed within four days. This requirement doubtless was designed to emphasize the commitment of the faculty to classroom teaching, often overlooked in graduate studies in those days, and was generally considered to be the most strenuous of the requirements.

This commitment to quality extends beyond the educational realm. In discussions with friends Clark identifies relevant issues and is quick to frame revealing questions. He musters from his great store of experience things that point to areas of consideration or explanations for circumstances. In a broader sense he always wants the best of everything for his friends. He is quick to mention an opportunity or point out something that he believes a friend would enjoy or that is in some way connected with something of interest.

One of Clark's notable and interesting practices relates to his meeting of new acquaintances. He tends to explore the interests and activities of the person with an eye to identifying the things that the newcomer might find interesting or useful. He then pursues the interests that he identifies, seeking both to widen his own knowledge and to place his own enormous store of information at the disposal of the new acquaintance.

All this is indicative of a related part of Clark's personality—he is very inquisitive. This applies to all aspects of his scholarly work and to every part of the physical and intellectual environment in which

he lives. This inquisitiveness knows no bounds. His historical interests are as wide as the human mind can imagine. Most historians have
limited areas of professional interest and spend their professional lives
exploring relatively small chronological and topical areas. But Clark's
professional interests are limitless—an early railroad, a state history,
the exploration of a river across time, southern newspaper editors, a
broad exploration of the American frontier, the role of country stores
in the southern economy and society, and many more topics that for
one reason or another he was drawn to explore. His mind seems always to be two or three projects beyond his involvement. And in his
contacts with friends and acquaintances he always has some contribution to make, some inquiry to pursue, some addition to make to
the communal interests, and some observation to expand one's understanding.

In Kentucky Clark has extended his concerns and activities beyond the bounds of the institution of which he was a part. To his
friends, acquaintances, and colleagues he has raised questions and
pushed actions relative to the state's economy. He joined others in
criticizing the impact of broad-form deeds, unrestricted strip mining,
and clear-cutting of old-growth timber and the erosion associated
with these practices. He raised the awareness of his friends and enlisted them in his activities aimed at salvaging some portion of the
state's resources before it was too late. In particular, he took a personal
role in forestry on both his own and others' land and earned citations
for his activities in this field.

Clark is deeply interested in other areas as well and has enlisted
his friends and colleagues in addressing these concerns. He joined
with other faculty members in building the holdings of the University of Kentucky Library and in building library facilities. Perhaps
more than any other single faculty member, Clark placed the University Archives in an operational condition. He assisted in dispatching

people into the field to visit most parts of the Commonwealth and contact local leaders to secure gifts of manuscripts to build the University Archives. He secured on his own initiative the massive collection of southern country store records. In the process he called on a growing circle of friends, acquaintances, and (in the later years) former students to gain the necessary support for these efforts, which were essential in building research holdings and contributed significantly to the conversion of the University of Kentucky into a research and graduate institution.

As Clark came to be known more and more extensively outside of the university circle as an active historian, a seeker of resources for the study of Kentucky, and a person deeply concerned with the improvement of the state, he used his increasing circle of friends (including a substantial number of political leaders) to gather, preserve, and make usable the great masses of historical material held by the numerous government bodies. His friends were easily brought into the fight for the preservation and housing of these materials, and almost axiomatically the supporters of these activities became, if they were not already, a part of the growing body of Clark's friends.

Another aspect of his character generates widespread support for Clark's opinions: he is extremely perceptive. This circumstance, combined with his broad exposure to diverse data, permits him to reach conclusions that almost always prove to be accurate and consequently persuasive. His friends and acquaintances long ago learned that even if his views were not wholly persuasive, they always narrowed the area of discussion dramatically. This perceptiveness is also notable in his research. Many of us have been frustrated by the rapidity with which he shapes his presentations on a variety of topics. Others of us plod along in search of conclusions while Clark's perceptive brilliance enables him to explain these topics with accuracy and understanding. I recall well when a friend of ours was researching a doctoral dissertation on the western Shaker movement. Clark had earlier published an account of the Pleasant Hill Shaker community as a chapter in his book *The Kentucky*. It was clear that Clark could not have had access to all of the sources that the student had, but as the student said— with admiration and some measure of frustration—"he is absolutely right about every significant thing." He and I have never (with one very minor exception) researched the same topics, but I have never doubted that, had we done so, Clark would have reached his conclusions in far less time than I. His friends who are also scholars are universally astounded and bemused by his perceptive insights.

But these observations should by no means be taken as suggestions that Clark's work is thin. That is clearly not the case. Indeed his publications are notable for the wealth of sources. His *Pills, Petticoats, and Plows* rests on an enormous volume of country store records. Even his more general works (clearly conceived as classroom textbooks) are heavily bolstered by lists of sources. The chapter notes of his *History of Kentucky* are notable, among other things, for extensive listings of contemporary newspapers. All of his friends and colleagues are well aware of the precision that marks everything Clark has ever done.

An interesting example of this precision can be seen in his woodworking. He has a great affection for wood and design. The huge freestanding map of Kentucky shaped from native woods that stands in the entryway of the Kentucky Archives and Records Building is a monument to his love for the material and the skill with which it can be worked. His scholarly works are also like this: sound materials shaped and joined with unsurpassed skill—nothing slighted and nothing shoddy. A neighbor of mine who was an extremely skilled furniture-maker in his spare time told me a story of an occasion at Boone Tavern in Berea. This inn is furnished with many pieces of local manufacture. My friend was drawn to a small table because he was unable to see how a certain jointure was made. Finally, he gave in and turned the table over to examine the construction. He heard a voice behind him saying, "I'm glad you did that. I've been wanting to see how they did that." It was, he subsequently learned, Tom Clark—seeking always and everywhere to find—and use—the most perfect way of putting the materials together to produce the best product. In one way or another probably each of his friends has experienced in diverse ways Clark's continuing search for the most nearly perfect way of assembling his materials—physical or intellectual. He is always eager to see what they have done and to admire their good craftsmanship as well.

However numerous the responsibilities placed upon Clark by his extensive obligations, they are never so burdensome as to separate him from his friends. His consideration for them is boundless. When a long-time colleague and close friend desperately wanted, in retirement, to revise and republish the major work of his career and was compelled by failing health to conclude that he could never accomplish this task, he asked Clark to finish the job he was unable to complete. Despite a very heavy burden of commitments, Clark agreed to undertake this additional chore. This is but a single example of the boundless consideration for his friends that is so much a part of his personality. Again and again he has undertaken actions for the benefit of his friends, often without any request.

Not so well known to casual acquaintances of Tom Clark is his sense of humor. This is notable in both his writings and his conversation. Indeed, almost every conversation is enlivened by humorous asides and observations. There was, for instance, the trip that he and his close friend and colleague James F. Hopkins took to inspect some timber acreage. Hopkins was universally known to his friends as "Hop," which their guide misheard as "Pop." This led to the guide's assumption that Hop was Clark's father and to a hilarious and extended interchange.

It is not possible for us really to understand Thomas D. Clark and the work he has done by examining that work alone. We can form some views of Clark in his various capacities—scholar, teacher, archivist, editor, professional association builder, political advocate, forester, and a dozen other venues. But to bring these concepts together and to fully understand any of them we must go beyond these achievements. We would wish to gain some real understanding of the nature of the man who is more than the sum of these accomplishments. For he has been driven by something broader and deeper than we can fathom. His commitment and sense of obligation transcend our own comprehension. We can only contemplate our friend's work with affection, respect, and awe.

Inspirer

JAMES DUANE BOLIN

From a sixth-floor office at a regional university in far western Kentucky, it is not difficult for a not-so-young historian in mid-career to be inspired again by Thomas D. Clark. Indeed, I am reminded of Clark whether I turn to scan bookshelves lined with his works published by a university press that he helped to found, or turn to framed photographs of Kentucky's historian laureate at a recent book fair in Frankfort, or to a posed book cover shot of a pensive Clark in "country gentleman" hat, no doubt considering the future grandeur of South Carolina or Kentucky tree seedlings newly planted. I am reminded of Clark when I encounter cherished notes scribbled out by his hand or typed on Clark's unmistakable antique typewriter. Even when I look down on the tops of mature willow oaks and sugar maples and white pines or the stately College of Education building across 16th Street, I remember his contributions—to conservation and education reform—beyond his chosen discipline of history.

Clark's scholarly contributions to the history of the American West and South and to Kentucky are inspirational—if not daunting—to lesser historians. When we consider his contributions outside the strict confines of the discipline, however, we encounter a servant historian whose concerns extend beyond his particular vocation or "calling." Clark has been critical of the idea of "calling" as an excuse for an uneducated, fundamentalist ministerial vocation. "Too many ministers preach the doctrine 'I don't have an education; I don't need an education to understand the "word of God" or to preach the "word of God,""" Clark stated in an interview with a western Kentucky attorney, "Calling" in this sense has been used as a justification for intellectual laziness.[1] Clark surely has made the discipline of history his "calling," however, and if anyone is called to be a historian—whether the caller be Clio or God—it is Clark. The poet Gerard Manley Hopkins wrote: "What I do is me: for that I came." Clark has inspired me to extend my particular "calling" to a more general "calling" of service in the discipline of history and beyond. After all, as the writer/theologian Frederick Buechner has written, "calling" should be the place where "our deep gladness and the world's deep hunger meet."[2]

It was a seventh-grade Kentucky history course that introduced me to a study of the state's past beyond family visits to the state capitol, state parks, and Civil War battlefields. Even then, my stern and caustic teacher threw around Clark's name as the fount of all commonwealth knowledge. We did not question Mr. Harding when he began a discussion with, "According to Thomas D. Clark. . . ." Our seventh-grade textbook was not Clark's *History of Kentucky* but Van Hook's *Kentucky Story*. And although Joseph O. Van Hook made no mention of Clark's early contributions to the study of Kentucky history or to the elementary textbook *Exploring Kentucky* that he coauthored with Lee Kirkpatrick, the superintendent of schools in Paris, it was Clark's name that we came to know. I became interested in history as a course of study in the seventh grade, and so a reverence for history and for Clark became intertwined, if not synonymous.

In high school an inspirational teacher encouraged me to take seriously my own "calling" to teach and do history, and so, after four years of basketball and books at a small liberal arts college in Tennessee and a year of graduate school in Texas, I returned to Kentucky, first to teach in western Kentucky public schools and then to complete graduate work at the University of Kentucky. In my third semester at

UK I was reintroduced to Clark's "legacy" when a consortium of groups sponsored a symposium and dinner in his honor on November 10, 1981. A collection of scholars, including many of the writers contributing essays to this latest tribute, paid homage to Clark's contributions to the study of southern, Kentucky, and western history. Representatives from the University Press of Kentucky, the Kentucky Historical Society, the Kentucky Department for Libraries and Archives, UK's Department of History, and the university's Special Collections and Archives all gave testimony to Clark's work in and for these various entities. George Brown Tindall capped off the evening with an address titled "History and the Future of the South."

While Clark has written on a wide range of topics, the fact that he reveres state and local history made a deep impression on me. When the physician poet William Carlos Williams wrote that "one does not have to be uninformed to consort with cows . . . the local is the only thing that is universal," he quoted from John Dewey. "The local is the only universal," Dewey said, and "upon that all art builds." "I wanted, if I was to write in a larger way than of the birds and flowers," Williams stated in his autobiography, "to write about the people close about me; to know in detail, minutely what I was talking about to the whites of their eyes, to their very smells."[3] Williams and Dewey could easily have been writing about Clark's sympathetic devotion to the nuances of local history, whether in a central Kentucky county or in scores of general stores throughout the South. In *Pills, Petticoats, and Plows* Clark turned vivid descriptions of southern merchants and general stores and those who frequented them into a revealing account of the effect of mercantile trade in the South and the economic revolution that would destroy the local economies on which the general stores thrived:

Down the center aisle past the public circle were racks
loaded with meal and flour in bags, salt, and feed. Piled up

behind these were odd lots of hardware. No space was wasted; plows, wagon spokes, buggy shafts, coils of rope, plowshares, axes, wedges, sledge hammers, rolls of bagging and ties were on open display where not too much effort was required to point them out to customers. Shopping for many goods became a matter of craning the neck around the whole store. Hanging from the ceiling were many crude but necessary utensils and tools of the everyday life in the rural South.[4]

Clark's devotion to detail and his work ethic in ferreting out those details continue to give young historians instruction in doing history. He admitted that "I'm one of the last walking-on-shoe-leather agrarian historians."[5] In researching his *Historic Maps of Kentucky,* published by the University Press of Kentucky in 1979, Clark, of course, delved into pertinent government documents, governors' papers, legislative acts, and survey plats. He consulted relevant reference works and secondary sources. And then, the "walking-on-shoe-leather" historian did something else. He drove from Lexington to southern Simpson County to fight through the brambles in search of engraved stones marking the "black jack jog," the odd indention in the Kentucky/Tennessee border. There he is, the seventy-five-year-old historian, with walking stick in hand, conducting his own survey of the disputed boundary. "I have made a considerable effort to locate some of these markers, and only in one case have I found one standing partially upright and virtually unharmed," Clark wrote in the preface that accompanied the maps.[6] Considerable effort indeed! As the poet Williams would have him, Clark described in *Pills, Petticoats, and Plows* the "very smells" of a general store, evoking a sense of the place. These evocations readers would not soon forget:

Above the commonplace everyday odors of the stores there
was a change. There was a much stronger overtone of
cheese. Oranges and apples gave a richness; burned powder
from fireworks added an acrid flavor and above all of this
was the fragrant bouquet of Bourbon or the raw tang of
corn whisky. Newly opened tubs of corned mackerel sat well
back out of range of careless tobacco chewers. Here was an
assortment of merchandise and rich smells which made
indelible impressions on several generations of southerners
and which is to many, even yet, a reminder of Christmas.[7]

Through Clark's work, these "indelible impressions" continue
into the present day. This was no nostalgic trip into a "misty, sentimentalized, mythical past," however.[8] No, the hardships of life for a
majority of southerners rang true as the agonizing, tortuous reality of
southern existence was not glossed over:

Securing a water supply in the country was a major physical
undertaking. . . . Nothing tested the fortitude of a southerner
just home from the spiritually revitalizing influences of a
camp meeting so much as drawing water barehanded for a
herd of thirsty cows. It was by the side of the back country
wells that much of southern womanhood lost both beauty
and health. There was none of the Old Testament romance
connected with these shallow sources of water below the
Mason and Dixon line.[9]

Such writing spoke to a western Kentucky boy whose pharmacist/
minister father could recall the very scenes described with such vitality in Clark's work. In "Walking Into the Past," western Kentucky
poet Ron Watson described the universal nature of the local in lines

that William Carlos Williams and Thomas D. Clark would understand:

Walking Into the Past

It's Saturday and we stop at the Dalton Store
before putting in on the river.
Oldtimers are holding down a bench
that hasn't changed in 20 years
and somebody shot Homer Bailey's dog
for running deer is what we hear
as the screen door squeaks open
and slams shut
and swallows us into the general store
that is always darker than outside.

A fading red Coke machine
is defining nostalgia against a wall
and kids we might have been
are standing on a footrail
at the counter. We hope
it is black licorice and Moon Pies
but they could be buying anything.

We try not to hurry
and for a moment begin to blend
as easy as shade into the slow scene,
to soak up the almost forgotten something
we once were.

Paid-up, the kids spill toward us
in a stream that we divide. We turn
to watch it reconnect down the dark aisle
that points like a chute in the cool dimness
toward a door that opens like a tablet of light.[10]

I associate the last stanza of Watson's poem with the lesson that Clark taught me through his books, and I have tried to picture a father and his small son standing hand in hand in the middle of the store's darkened aisle soaking in "the almost forgotten something we once were." Standing in the present, the father and son gaze into the darkened interior at "kids we might have been" at a counter buying perhaps "black licorice and Moon Pies," only to have the representative group from the past "spill toward us in a stream that we divide." And even as the past comes hurtling into and through the present, the familial pair "turn to watch it reconnect" into the future "toward a door that opens like a tablet of light." These "connecting links between our ancestors and ourselves," in the words of John Egerton— links among the past, present, and future—have surely become evident in the long and fruitful life of Thomas D. Clark.[11] "As far as we're concerned, there's no such thing as a dead past," Clark told an interviewer in 2001. "That's the wrong connotation. You're part of the past. Everything you do, everything you touch in some way has an intimate association with the past. No matter what you do . . . in any area of human activity, it has a direct relation all the way back to the past." "Even human prejudices are age-old," Clark emphasized. "It's important to understand where some of these things came from."[12]

In our graduate school carrels on the seventeenth floor of UK's Patterson Office Tower, we teaching assistants heard the stories of the history department's glory days. Ensconced in Frazee Hall, the likes of Clement Eaton and Holman Hamilton and Albert D. Kirwan had been assembled under the leadership of department chair Clark. We reveled in the various renditions of faculty foibles and department politics. We experienced vicariously the fear or anger of a graduate student or indeed a faculty member whose scholarship had fallen short of the glory, or at least of the high expectations, of the department head. Clark served as department chair from 1942 until 1965, when President John W. Oswald put in place a system of rotating chairmanships. That year the department's Phi Alpha Theta chapter held a banquet to honor Clark's tenure as chair. Kirwan gave eloquent tribute to Clark's service to the department and to the discipline in his address "You Made Us What We Are Today":

> I was here at the University, although in an unrelated field of endeavor, when Tom Clark assumed leadership of the history department. He was a young man, then, not long out of the Mississippi prairie country, a young man with unbounded self-confidence, yet with a sense of deep humility; one with an almost superhuman capacity of work and concentration, yet with an effervescent good humor and overpowering sense of comedy. He took charge of a department which hardly deserved the name. . . .
>
> I think you will agree with me, then, that the record indicates that our chairman has built this, the strongest department in this University, and one of the truly distinguished history departments in the country, at a time when he has himself been setting the pace, establishing a reputation for himself as one of the most eminent of the country's historians.[13]

Clark's legacy was secure. The department delivered a chair to Clark's home, symbolic of the newly designated Theodore Hallam Chair that he would hold until he "retired" in 1968. "And in the coming years, when you will no longer have to be burdened with administering the details of the department," Kirwan remarked, "we want you to just sit in it and relax and reflect."[14] Unlike most retired professors, however, Clark refused to sit quietly in his study or putter around his yard on Tahoma Road. Instead, years of greater productivity were ahead, and it has been in those three and a half decades that he has inspired me and yet another generation of historians.

From the beginning of his teaching career—when he taught five classes each semester—Clark believed strongly that, for historians, teaching and research must complement each other. Can research and writing advance teaching? Clark responded without hesitation: "Yes, sir. It gives you a certainty about things. It gives you a perspective about the whole business of historical criticism and historical evaluation. It develops a critical eye. Finally, research can be humbling in that it reveals how little you really know about a subject."[15]

In *The Pleasures* of *Academe: A Celebration and Defense of Higher Education*, published in 1998, James Axtell wrote about the multifaceted lives of university teachers. In chapters titled "Confessions of a Bibliolater," "(Mis)Understanding Academic Work," "What Makes a University Great," and "Scholarship Reconsidered," Axtell identifies the many "pleasures of academe."[16] Chief among them, according to Axtell, is the opportunity to teach even beyond the classroom. Axtell could have used Thomas D. Clark as a case study.

In his chapter "Twenty-five Reasons to Publish," Axtell argues that the impact of the teacher who ignores research and writing "is exclusively local, unlike the scholar's, which may be national or international." Students "need to see, through living example, that education is a continuing experience." They need to know that while professors preach the value and necessity of history, they practice what they preach by doing history themselves. Axtell quoted Louis B. Wright, who after years of giving out Huntington Library fellowships, concluded that "if research had no other value, its service in keeping professors alive and interested in their fields of knowledge would amply justify it." Let's face it: "Many students will soon forget the details and even general themes of their college courses, but few will forget the passion with which their professors approached the subject day after day or the inspiration they gave them to think the subject important and worth pursuing."[17]

In a 1987 interview, Clark gave sound advice about writing: "I would say to historians, generally, and young historians in particular, that I think the writing of history for the most part should be clear, it should be simplistic in style, and at the same time it should be factual and objective."[18] Clark warned that writing can be mysterious, lonely work. "In all my teaching career, I have never been able to solve a mystery," he told the interviewer. "I would sit at the typewriter or with a lapboard and work on a manuscript and get it written out in some fashion in a draft, and then I would take the draft to the typewriter and type it, and get it out as clean and clear as I could, and go at it again." "I don't think I've ever had a book that hasn't gone through at least six or seven drafts, and that means a lot of work—a lot of paper and a lot of lonely nights. Writing is a lonely business," he said. Clark wanted young historians to know what they were getting into: "Good writing is hard, sweaty work."[19]

So Thomas D. Clark has inspired me to take my "calling," in all of its manifestations, seriously. Historians teach and write, but servant historians of Clark's ilk go beyond the classroom and the study. And if we are to use Clark as an example, it is after retirement from university responsibilities that the real work begins. Clark has shattered my comfortable dreams of a peaceful and restful retirement. I had visions, should I live into retirement, of puttering across the campus at my university on an early fall afternoon, freed from committee meetings, workshops, and essay grading. I would admire the brilliant fall colors, the rows of sugar maples in the quadrangle, nod at the statue of the university's founder, and, holding onto the handrail, make my way into the cool interior of Pogue Library to lose myself in the stacks or at a dark wooden table, taking notes or napping in antiquarian delight. Clark anticipated his own retirement activities when he said, "In retirement you have to be careful about planning ahead of time what you are going to do or you will waste away all your time."[20] So much for nodding and napping in Pogue Library's reading room. I hope Clark is happy that he has ruined my retirement reverie!

The quantity and range of Clark's retirement activities are staggering. He has continued to publish book after book, with *The People's House: Governor's Mansions of Kentucky*, as his latest offering. "When 'mere' professors retire," James Axtell wrote, "they often find themselves at loose ends without an audience, the applause and responsiveness of a class, or the daily routine of teaching, however much they may have complained of the 'rat race' during the school year." Like Clark, however, "habitual scholars, by contrast, make easier transitions because they always have their reading, research, and writing which, if arteriosclerosis doesn't set in prematurely, should be as good as, or better than, the work they produced on the job."[21]

Clark's retirement activities have gone beyond the publication of books. He has written enough blurbs for the dust jackets of other scholars' books to fill yet another volume. A founder of the University of Kentucky Press in 1943, he helped found the new consortium, the University Press of Kentucky in 1968. He taught at Indiana University, where he wrote a multivolume history of that institution, and still later at Eastern Kentucky University, the University of Wisconsin, and Winthrop College. A coveted speaker, he has accepted invitations from scores of universities, libraries, and the Kentucky General Assembly. In 1991 I heard him address members of a Leadership Academy at Shakertown in Mercer County on the topic "Why We Are Where We Are in Kentucky." He has befriended the Kentucky Oral History Commission and the Kentucky Humanities Council. He helped make the Kentucky History Center a reality and is now working to remake the old Fayette County Courthouse into a Lexington history museum and arts center. His efforts to secure a new Kentucky constitution have been unsuccessful, however.

In 2002, he found time to accompany the new director of the University Press of Kentucky to western Kentucky in order to introduce him to a sometimes neglected part of the state. Who better to point out the rich diversity of the commonwealth than the ninety-nine-year-old author of *Kentucky: Land of Contrast*, published in 1968, the year he "retired" from the University of Kentucky?[22]

After returning to Kentucky following a sojourn at a small liberal arts college in Arkansas, I seemed to see Clark or hear about him everywhere I turned. Even in Arkansas, brackets on the front wall of my classroom held a collection of maps, "Cram's Superior Series, Historical School Maps (American Made)." The "Current Editor," with his name prominently displayed in the lower right-hand corner of each map, was "Thomas D. Clark, Ph.D., Distinguished Professor of American History, Emeritus, University of Kentucky, Lexington, Kentucky." Once back in Kentucky, I would see him at the University Press of Kentucky booth at annual meetings of the Southern Historical Association, in magazines or on television, or at annual meetings of the Kentucky Association of Teachers of History (KATH). He spoke at KATH meetings in 1988 and 1992, but in 1996 the whole conference at Centre College in Danville was given over to "Dr. Thomas D. Clark, Historian and Citizen: A Celebration of Service." The conference honored the servant historian.

It is his individual attention that has inspired me most, and two specific examples of his beneficence serve as models for other historians to consider and emulate. In 1998, I drove—with my nine-year-old son in tow—on a research trip, first to Louisville and then to Lexington to talk with Clark about Kentucky history. We traveled the familiar succession of parkways and interstates from Murray in far western Kentucky in a small pick-up truck with room only for the two of us and bags of books and clothes. Wesley read (it was Tolkien's *The Fellowship of the Ring* on this trip), looking up from time to time to get his bearings and talk for a while about school or books or whatever.

My son had already met Clark at an annual meeting of the Kentucky Historical Society in Frankfort, and when Wesley asked him to sign his program, Clark signed his hand instead. Wesley refused to wash his hand afterward until finally the autograph wore away and only the memory remained. Now, after arriving in Lexington we made our ritual trek to a Lexington bookstore, and then before driving back west to Murray we stopped at Clark's home, on the appropriately named Kentucky Avenue, next to Woodland Park.

Mrs. Clark ushered us down a hallway to a pleasant, light-filled room where we sat at a round table and waited for Dr. Clark to join us. After introducing my son again to the great man and asking permission to record the interview, I pushed a button on the machine and posed a question. There ensued a conversation that lasted almost two hours. In the one interview, Kentucky's historian laureate doled out nuggets on Kentucky politics (his personal remembrances of Lexington's early twentieth-century political boss); the influence of Baptists on the history of Kentucky (including a firsthand account of "old man Porter," the influential, controversial pastor of Lexington's First Baptist Church); and the significance and contribution of Adolph Rupp to college basketball and also his place in the university community. In two hours and one fell swoop I had recorded an interview that informed all three research projects with which I was then engaged. A productive session, to say the least. But the real value of that afternoon's verbal ramble with the Kentucky historian went beyond my own narrow research interests. Although Wesley seemed to be preoccupied with a large vase containing a small pine branch perched at the center of the round table, he drank it all in.

As we rose to take our leave, Clark, ever the teacher, quizzed us on the variety of pine in the vase. We failed the quiz. After muttering the name of the only pine species that I knew—white pine—Clark dismissed the response and calmly gave the proper name of the long-needled variety on display. He walked us to the door, but not before Mrs. Clark had given us a copy of her history of the Lexington Woman's Club. (I had mentioned that one of my graduate students was working on the woman's club movement in Kentucky for a master's thesis.) Dr. Clark had written a preface for his wife's fine book.

A year later, my friend and former high school history teacher and I traveled to Lexington because Clark had told us about a rich nine-teenth-century diary in the holdings of the university's Special Collections, the manuscripts library that he founded and developed while chair of the history department. As a young professor he had persuaded a granddaughter to give her grandfather's diary to the library. He insisted that he show us the diary firsthand. We drove directly to Clark's house. He was ready when we arrived, and somehow we all three squeezed into the only seat to be had in the small pickup truck. We rolled down the windows and made our way to UK's Special Collections.

We walked—Clark with a cane—from a parking lot to a back door of the library, stopping several times, not to rest, certainly, but to chat with students and acquaintances he encountered. Inside the building we meandered through maze-like corridors—the library was under construction for renovations—and found our way to an information desk where Clark told the manuscripts librarian what he needed. My teacher and I sat at a long wooden table and waited for the treasure to arrive, while Clark went off in search of other materials for his own research. When the worker brought four large gray manuscript boxes containing the handwritten diary to our table, both of us took up a box to begin reading the minuscule script. The diarist had lived through much of the nineteenth century. The diary had not been transcribed.

With one look at the large boxes and at the stacks of handwritten pages, previous historians had surely been frightened away, understanding all the while the historical rewards awaiting someone willing to devote patience and hard work to the task. After some time, Clark surprised us at the table, opened up a gray box, turned over a few pages, and said, "Now, we'll see what kind of historians you are."

Well, now. We have yet to make use of the diary, with its treasure trove of insight into the antebellum, Civil War, and postwar periods of American history. We do not yet know what kind of historians we are or what kind we may become. We do know the kind of historian who has shown us the way: a servant historian willing, in his late nineties, to take up the whole of an afternoon to pry himself into the seat of a 1992 Ford Ranger truck, to walk two historians up to a neglected primary source, and to issue a challenge that the two will never forget.

NOTES

1. Bill Cunningham, *Kentucky's Clark* (Kuttawa, Ky.: McClanahan Publishing, 1987), 98.

2. Frederick Buechner, *Wishful Thinking: A Theological ABC* (New York: Harper and Row, 1973), 95. The Gerard Manley Hopkins line is from "As Kingfishers catch fire."

3. William Carlos Williams, *The Autobiography of William Carlos Williams* (New York: New Directions, 1967), 391.

4. Thomas D. Clark, *Pills, Petticoats, and Plows* (Indianapolis: Bobbs-Merrill, 1944), 48-49. Excerpts from this book were also included in a booklet "Printed for the friends, associates and admirers of Dr. Thomas D. Clark by Katherine Andrews, Patrice Carroll, Deborah Kessler, Marcie Sledd, Marshall White and Melanie White while participating in a work-

shop at The King Library Press under the direction of Gay Reading in the fall of 1981."

5. Ted Sloan, "Eyewitness to History," *Kentucky Monthly* (July 2001), 13.

6. Thomas D. Clark, *Historic Maps of Kentucky* (Lexington: Univ. Press of Kentucky, 1979), v.

7. Clark, *Pills, Petticoats, and Plows,* 124-25.

8. This phrase was given to me by historian Kenneth Moore Startup, vice president for Academic Affairs, Williams Baptist College, Walnut Ridge, Arkansas.

9. Clark, *Pills, Petticoats, and Plows,* 49.

10. Ron Watson, "Walking into the Past," poem given as a gift to the author, 21 Sept. 1990.

11. John Egerton, *Generations: An American Family* (New York: Simon & Schuster, 1983), 14.

12. Sloan, "Eyewitness to History," 14.

13. Frank Furlong Mathias, Albert D. Kirwan (Lexington: Univ. Press of Kentucky, 1975), 99, 101.

14. Ibid., 202.

15. Cunningham, *Kentucky's Clark,* 146.

16. See James Axtell, *The Pleasures of Academe: A Celebration and Defense of Higher Education* (Lincoln: Univ. of Nebraska Press, 1998).

17. Ibid., 55, 59, 60, 61.

18. Cunningham, *Kentucky's Clark,* 120.

19. Ibid., 120, 121.

20. Ibid., 149.

21. Axtell, *Pleasures of Academe,* 57.

22. See Thomas D. Clark, *Kentucky: Land of Contrast* (New York: Harper & Row, 1968).

Mentor

Edward M. Coffman

Thomas D. Clark is recognized as one of Kentucky's major cultural assets and throughout his long career, he has taught and influenced thousands of students. It was my privilege to be one of the relative few who worked with him as both an undergraduate and graduate student. Having him as a mentor for more than fifty years has certainly been to my great advantage as a scholar and teacher.

On a crisp January day in 1949, I was among some two hundred students crowding into the large classroom on the third floor of Frazee Hall at the University of Kentucky. It was the beginning of the semester and this was the first meeting of the History of Kentucky course. I looked forward to this class because I was interested in the subject and knew the teacher's reputation through articles about and by him in the *Louisville Courier-Journal*.

As the students settled down, a handsome, solidly built man strode vigorously into the room, quickly got through the necessary administrative business of a first class meeting, and began to talk about history. Within minutes I knew I was listening to one of the best lecturers I had ever heard. His voice carried well without electrical amplification to those of us in the back of the room, while his accent (a blend of Mississippi and Kentucky) was pleasant. His style varied with the topic at hand from dynamic to a slower paced storytelling mode. I don't remember if he had notes that day. In that class and in others he sometimes carried notes, but I don't recall his referring to them. He was authoritative with an impressive command of the facts seasoned with a sense of humor and a lot of common sense. I was in awe of him. As a twenty-year-old sophomore, however, I had no idea that he would become a major influence in my life for more than half a century. That was my first encounter with Thomas D. Clark.

Over that spring semester, as he spanned the rich and colorful history of Kentucky, he covered the heroes and the scoundrels and gave notable events their due, but he also talked about the ordinary folk—those who pioneered and their descendants who peopled the farms and villages. One could almost hear the ring of axes felling trees and feel the push of a plow behind a mule. There were also the tall stories that had enlivened many a gathering around the wood-fired pot-bellied stove in a country store. In sum, we learned about a way of life as well as the names, events, and dates that one expected in a history class.

The course required a short term paper on a local history topic. I had known and admired a local National Guard officer in my home-town of Hopkinsville, so I asked and got Clark's approval to write about him. I talked with the man's widow and corresponded with a Regular Army officer who had worked with him before World War I, but I leaned primarily on a biographical sketch and assorted other mentions in Charles M. Meacham's *A History of Christian County, Kentucky, from Oxcart to Airplane* (1930). As a final touch I painstak-ingly tried to copy by hand the photo of my subject for a frontispiece.

I can't find that term paper now, but I recall that Clark liked it, although he wanted me to add footnotes. He followed up with a re-quest to check the Hopkinsville newspaper for mention of another National Guard officer during the Spanish-American War mobiliza-tion. When I sent the relevant quotation to him in early June, he re-sponded with a note that encouraged me to major in history "because you show real promise in the field."[1] Naturally I was very pleased with the compliment, but I continued in my journalism major. I liked history very much but I had my doubts that I could make a living as a historian. Besides, only one other Hopkinsvillian, to my knowledge, had been a history scholar. He published two books, then, as the local librarian told me, he went mad.

The next fall I enrolled in History of the New South, which met in a regular sized classroom on Frazee's second floor. Again I enjoyed Clark's lectures as he described the trials and tribulations of the post–Civil War South. One morning as he was explaining the tenancy system and the crop liens that kept those farmers in bondage, he dashed out to his office next door and brought back a handful of yellowed scraps of paper—original crop liens. As he shook them in his fist, he talked of the long hours of toil and the debts that mounted every year—the miseries and heartbreaks these pieces of paper represented. If anyone in that room did not have historical imagination before that lecture, they certainly got it with that dramatic illustration.

There was an authenticity in those lectures on the New South. While Clark did not refer to personal experiences, he obviously knew firsthand about many of his subjects. After all, he had lived through much of the period. As I learned later from Holman Hamilton's biographical sketch, Clark had been born in a log house in rural Mississippi, had farmed cotton, corn, and sugar cane, had worked in a sawmill and on a river dredge. The social, economic, and political milieu of the early twentieth century rural South was the stuff and framework of his life.[2]

The Korean War broke out while I was at ROTC Camp at Fort Benning in June 1950. I no longer had to worry about choosing a career or making a living because I was called up soon after graduation in 1951. During my first year in the army, I decided that I really wanted to be a historian. I assumed that I could save up enough from my second lieutenant's pay to cover expenses for a year in graduate school, and that after I earned a master's degree I could teach in high school and save enough to work on a doctorate. Actually I knew nothing about graduate programs except I had heard that it was better not to continue at your undergraduate school. Since I had not been a history major, however, I thought I would return to Kentucky for the master's work and then go to Duke for a Ph.D. I knew that Clark and Dr. Albert D. Kirwan, the only two history teachers I had had as an undergraduate, had earned their doctorates at Duke.

In the spring of 1953, while in Japan, I wrote to Clark about my desire to enter the graduate program that fall. He promptly responded, "We will be very happy to have you." He added that they did not have financial aid immediately available but he was sure there would be in the "near future."[3] I was elated and not worried about money at that point, since the recently enacted Korean War G.I. Bill eased my financial concerns.

Almost two years in the infantry had whetted my desire to get back to classes. I found the other entering graduate students— Leonard Curry, Paul Taylor, and Richard Trautman—congenial and the experienced ones—Monroe Billington, Holman Hamilton, Dwight Mikkelson, and David Wells—helpful.[4] It took only the initial class meetings to make me realize that I had a heavy course load. Three lecture courses and a seminar meant a lot of reading.

Throughout my graduate school days, Clark was always ready to advise and help when needed. A visit to his office was an experience. A small room on the second floor of Frazee Hall housed both his office and the department secretary's. One entered the secretary's space, which was separated by a half glass partition with an open entry on her right, from Clark's office. If memory serves me, his space was some six by twelve feet, furnished with his desk against the partition, a desk chair, a visitor's chair, a couple of bookcases, and books, journals, and papers that covered almost all of the area. There was a large window facing Limestone Street and overlooking trees in front of the Student Union, but one got the impression that Clark rarely gazed out of that window. After clearing away books and papers from the extra chair, I would bring up my question or problem. The answers were always direct and helpful and wound up with a strong dose of encouragement. I always remember leaving his office charged up with inspiration to do what needed to be done. Work hard and the results will be good.

I had come to graduate school with one preconceived idea—I wanted to write about Thomas H. Hines and the Northwest Conspiracy during the Civil War. As a senior, shortly before graduation, I had heard that the Hines Papers were in the library's Special Collections, and I had gone to the fourth floor of the Margaret I. King Library to look at them. There was a fascinating story in Hines's efforts to raise a Copperhead revolt in Illinois, Indiana, and Ohio and free the thousands of Confederate prisoners of war in the fall of 1864. This was the research topic I proposed in the seminar, and Clark and Merton England, who team-taught the class, approved this topic, which I later expanded into my master's thesis.

The lessons I carried away from that seminar were the need to use to the fullest extent original sources and to be accurate in the portrayal of people and events. One should consult secondary works but depend on the primary sources to find out what happened. Reading Civil War newspapers set the background for my topic. The bias and misinformation became clear as I paged through hundreds upon hundreds of issues. Such an immersion not only provided data but steeped me in the flavor of the era. More exciting were the contents of the two boxes of Hines Papers. There were letters, a fragmentary diary, a map of Chicago that Hines needed for his plan to liberate the POWs at Camp Douglas, and even a small saw that he had smuggled into a prison.

My second year, I took the two-semester lecture course in the

American Frontier. Again I was enthralled by Clark's lectures as he vividly depicted the dangers, hardships, and occasional rollicking good times of pioneers. I don't remember what I wrote about in the second semester term paper, but I tackled the First American Regiment on the frontier from August 1784 to January 1786 for my fall semester topic. This served as my introduction to the Lyman C. Draper collection which the library had recently purchased on microfilm, I assume on Clark's recommendation. What an unforgettable experience it was to read the letters, memoirs, and interviews of men who served in that regiment during those trying days!

In the spring of my second year I became engaged. I worried a bit about what Clark might say, since my concentration on history had been less than complete. I brought Anne to the Phi Alpha Theta banquet, and introduced her to him. His comment was that he had seen me several times with her and thought I looked like a "tom turkey building a nest in a fence corner." Some weeks later, at the history department picnic, Mrs. Clark talked with both of us about the long hours of work we could expect. She told us that after a full day at school with classes and the administrative duties of a department chairman, her husband would come home, have dinner, and then work from eight to midnight on his scholarship.

At the time I was not thinking far enough ahead to be concerned about my work schedule as a teacher and scholar. The formidable doctoral preliminary exams loomed on my immediate horizon. After months of study beyond the classroom requirements, I started the month-long slate of tests. During that period I had to take written exams in five fields—American History before and after 1865, Modern European History, English History, and American Literature—then wind up with an oral examination by all five professors.

Clark's students—and virtually all of us in the American history graduate program were his students—also had an additional requirement of writing four lectures in one four-day period sometime within that month. This tested one's ability and stamina to research, assimilate, organize, and write four nine- or ten-page papers, each with a bibliography, while under a good deal of pressure. It was a practical introduction to what we would have to do once we were teaching, although surely we would not be under the additional pressure of the prelim at any future time. Late in the afternoon of the fourth day, after a rather busy time, I turned in all four at the history office.

On a bright, rather warm December afternoon I reported for the oral exam at the history department, which was then temporarily located in Funkhouser Biological Science Building.[5] I had heard that the oral would not be difficult if one had done well on the written exams. That morning the secretary, Neva Armstrong (later Mrs. Ben Wall), phoned to tell me that I had done well. I was further relieved when Clark and Enno Kraehe, who tested me in European history, were most encouraging before the exam began. The oral turned out to be an interesting conversation about the several aspects of history and literature that the examiners represented. Needless to say, Christmas was very happy that year.

Although I knew that some people fell by the wayside even after they passed the great hurdle of prelims, I was not as worried about completing the dissertation. Holman Hamilton, who overlapped a year with me in graduate school and then stayed on as a faculty member, had summed up researching and writing the dissertation as a matter of applying the seat of the pants to the seat of the chair, whereas prelims had more possibility of failure, as one might have lapses of memory at a critical time or collapse under the pressure.

I decided to work on Peyton C. March as Chief of Staff of the army during World War I. March was a significant figure and, as far as I knew, no other historians were working on the American participation in World War I. I knew that this would mean a good deal of time in Washington, D.C., because I would have to go through March's papers and related collections in the Library of Congress as well as the War Department records in the National Archives.

Clark promptly approved my choice. Later I heard that there had been discussion at a departmental faculty meeting as to whether I should be allowed to do such a topic, which would call for so much research time in Washington. Since the department did not have travel expense money for graduate student research, students were encouraged to write on Kentucky or related topics, which could be researched in the collections that Clark and Ben Wall had gathered over the years. Clark never hinted at that discussion or discouraged me in any way from attempting the subject I had chosen. I did receive a relatively large fellowship, which I am certain he played a key role in obtaining. This, together with the G.I. Bill stipend and the hope of staying with a relative or friend in Washington, I believed, would tide me through the research.

My initial stint of three months in Washington made it clear that I would not be able to finish before the G.I. Bill and the fellowship ran out, so I began to look for a teaching job. In those days when academic jobs were not advertised, one had to depend on the major professor to hear about a job as well as for a recommendation. Here, Clark students were at a great advantage, since Thomas D. Clark was not only highly respected for his scholarship but also widely known for his leadership roles in professional associations and his many visiting professorships. But the job market in 1957 was very tough. I recall hearing about only one job from Clark—to teach an upper division course in American Economic History and four sections of American History survey at Memphis State University. Although I had never had economic history, I believed that my background in American history was solid enough to enable me to handle the upper division class as well as the surveys. Besides I needed a job—so I applied but heard nothing for several months. Finally, in mid-June, Enoch Mitchell, the head of the history department at MSU, got in touch with me through Clark and asked me to meet him at the Tennessee State Archives in Nashville for an interview—at my expense. On the basis of a brief face-to-face meeting and, much more, on Clark's recommendation, I was hired on the spot.

The next year, Dr. Clark recommended me for a fellowship that enabled me to spend a year completing my research and writing my dissertation. He approved it and shepherded me through the final oral examination. After another year at Memphis State, a year as Forrest C. Pogue's research assistant in his work on the first volume of his George C. Marshall biography, Pogue told me that the University of Wisconsin was searching for a military historian. In December I went to the American Historical Association meeting in New York City in hopes of making contact with people from the University of Wisconsin. There I ran into Clark, who was talking with another man. We exchanged pleasantries and I asked if he knew anyone from Wisconsin. As it happened, the man he was with was Vernon Carstensen, who not only taught there but was on the search committee. He suggested that I contact the chairman of the department, William Sachse, who was interviewing candidates. I phoned Bill, got an interview, and spent a half hour talking about my scholarly interests.

A couple of weeks later, I was asked to come to Madison. Bill and Nancy Sachse invited me to dinner, and afterwards the members of the search committee interviewed me.[6] The next morning I went to Bascom Hall and met and talked with several of the faculty in their offices. In what must have been a unique situation, my major professor sat in with the faculty group that I met with later that day. He had just come to Madison as a visiting professor that semester. A few days later, Bill Sachse telegraphed me an offer, which I promptly accepted.

Early in my second year at Madison, Oxford University Press gave me a contract to do a history of American participation in World War I. I excitedly wrote Clark the good news. His response set the tone of support and encouragement that remained constant in our meetings and correspondence over the years. First, he acknowledged my news: "I will be prouder of your book than you will be when it comes out." Then he continued: "I have good reports on you at Wisconsin. I knew when I recommended you so strongly to them that I was not taking any chance."[7] His comments on my books were always very heartening. He said that I wrote as if I knew the people. That was the standard of authenticity he had set and that I tried to attain.[8]

After he retired from UK, Clark went to Indiana University, where he also served as executive secretary of the Organization of American Historians. In that position he recommended me for the interesting assignment of representing the OAH for four years on the National Historical Publications Commission.[9] The quarterly meetings in which the Commission, chaired by the Archivist of the United States, discussed and voted on the funding of letterpress and microfilm editions of manuscript collections afforded me a broader view of history as well as acquaintance with the other commissioners. These visits also gave me the opportunity to do research at the National Archives about the Regular Army.

Early in 1984 Clark asked me to serve as the presenter for the OAH's Distinguished Service award at the annual convention. No one deserved such an award more than he. In addition to service on various committees over the years, he had been president and executive secretary and had even helped rename the organization. It was an honor to be asked. I gave a brief talk that summarized his accomplishments and emphasized his contributions as a scholar and teacher. At other conventions we had often met and chatted in hotel lobbies as other friends joined in, but on this occasion we had a long private conversation in which he reminisced about his early life and discussed historians and writers he had known.[10]

After retiring in 1992, my wife and I decided to return to Lexington. Clark responded to this with a welcoming note: "I look forward to your coming home." After our arrival, he invited me to lunch at the Faculty Club and, at the age of ninety-one, drove me there. At that time he asked me if there was anything he could do for me and I said I would like a user's card at the university library. He walked there with me and went to the director's office and got a card on the spot. I was now ready to do more research.

Aging has not been a period of decline for Clark. When he turned ninety, he wrote me that he "was still trying to be a historian." What an understatement! He still wrote and published books and maintained a schedule that would have wilted most men fifty years his junior as he continued his research and writing in addition to traveling throughout the state to give talks and attend committee meetings.

At the fiftieth reunion of the class of 1951, in October 2001, he drove to the Alumni Club, talked with various alumni, and then joined us for breakfast—where he refused to take the elevator and walked steadily down the stairs. After chatting throughout breakfast, he got up and gave a forty-minute talk about the University of Kentucky during the period when we were undergraduates. He used no notes and spoke as vigorously as ever as he enthralled the audience and regaled us with stories about the people and events of our youth—but his middle age. I could have closed my eyes and thought I was a student back in Frazee Hall.

The most important lesson Clark emphasized in his classes is that history is about people—not overarching theories, trends, or statistics—but "the crooked timber of humanity,"[11] the frontiersman breaking trail to a new beginning, the tenant farmer struggling to earn his family's subsistence on a small piece of land, the country storekeeper trying to balance his books, the small-town newspaper editor balancing the problem of telling the truth and making a living. In his lectures and writings, his enthusiasm for his subject is infectious as he stirs the historical imagination and brings alive the humanity of these people in all their strengths and weaknesses.

At the same time he held students to high standards of research and accuracy. Although he was demanding and strict in his standards, he was also flexible. At a time when graduate student mentors often demanded that their students be disciples as they assigned research topics within the limits of their own research interest, Clark recognized my interest in military history and let me pursue this. Throughout all of those years he was encouraging as he recommended me for fellowships and jobs and praised my scholarly efforts.

Thomas D. Clark is a model historian, and I am as much in awe of my mentor today as I was more than fifty years ago.

NOTES

1. Thomas D. Clark to Edward M. Coffman, June 14, 1949

2. Holman Hamilton, "Introduction," in Holman Hamilton, ed., *Three American Frontiers: Writings of Thomas D. Clark* (Lexington, Ky., 1968), ix-xiv.

3. Thomas D. Clark to Edward M. Coffman, May 11, 1953.

4. Herbert Finch, F. Gerald Ham, Frank Mathias, Thomas Nall, Claude Sturgill, and John Wilz entered the program later.

5. Earlier that year, in January 1956, a fire in Frazee Hall necessitated the relocating of offices and classrooms.

6. In addition to Sachse and Carstensen, they were Bill Hesseltine and Chester V. Easum.

7. Thomas D. Clark to Edward M. Coffman, Oct. 4, 1962.

8. Thomas D. Clark to Edward M. Coffman, March 11, 1966, May 21, 1987, and Jan. 6, 1990.

9. While I was on the Commission, its mandate was expanded to in-

clude publication of local and state documents, and the name was changed to National Historical Publications and Records Commission.

10. Thomas D. Clark to Edward M. Coffman, Feb. 6 and June 10, 1984.

11. The quotation is Isaiah Berlin's version of Immanuel Kant's phrase. Isaiah Berlin, *The Crooked Timber of Humanity: Chapters in the History of Ideas* (New York, 1991), 19.

Part V. The Works

Bibliographic Essay

Lowell H. Harrison

Abbreviations Used

AH	*American Heritage*
AHR	*American Historical Review*
FCHQ	*Filson Club Historical Quarterly*
IMH	*Indiana Magazine of History*
JAH	*Journal of American History*
JSH	*Journal of Southern History*
MVHR	*Mississippi Valley Historical Review*
Register	*Register of the Kentucky Historical Society*

Books

Thomas D. Clark is by a wide margin the most productive historian Kentucky has ever had. His first book was published in 1933; his most recent work appeared in November 2002. He insists that he was never motivated by a "publish or perish" edict; he has been active in researching and writing because of his creative urge. When he has encountered a subject that needed attention, he has accepted the challenge of doing something about it. In an extended interview with Bill Cunningham, Clark discussed some aspects of his philosophy of writing.

I think the writing of history for the most part should be a literary undertaking. By that, I mean it should be clear, it should be simplistic in style, and at the same time it should be factual and objective. I have never seen any fault or had any objection to a historian adding color so long as he does it with subtle touches. . . . Writing is a lonely business, but I have from the start determined that what I wrote was going to have some style. If I had any capability at all, I was going to give it some style.[1]

Without writing, I never would have had two precious experiences. One was the thrill and the exhilaration of making discoveries, of turning up some information that had never been used before and throwing some light on a subject that has some significance. The other, I felt that when I got into the classroom I could add an extra element of interest to the subject at hand, because I had a better understanding of the interpretation and the application of criticism that I never could have gotten without research and writing.[2]

Clark's writings have been quite diverse. As early chapters in this volume indicate, his major areas of interest have been Kentucky, the frontier, especially the old frontier east of the Mississippi, and the South, with emphasis on the post–Civil War era. He has had little interest in the Civil War except for its influence on the South after 1865. He has edited a number of works that supplement his own writings.

During his teaching years, Clark did most of his writing at home at night. His daughter recalls his working in his study, sometimes using a lapboard that he had made, but he never closed the door to exclude her and her brother. He usually took notes on half sheets of paper; index cards were used for bibliography and indexing. When he turned to the typewriter, he employed a rapid two-finger technique. Five or six drafts were needed as he added and deleted from the manuscript. In recent years he has depended more on Xeroxing to take care of notes. His goal throughout the writing process has been to create a readable, interesting product. Those terms appear frequently in the reviews of his books, from the first to the most recent.

Clark did his dissertation at Duke University in 1932 on "The Development of Railways in the Southwestern and Adjacent States before 1860," and that background influenced the publication of his first two books and several articles. *The Beginnings of the L&N: The Development of the Louisville and Nashville Railroad and Its Memphis Branches from 1836 to 1860* (Louisville, 1933), was his first. His second trip on the rails was *A Pioneer Southern Railroad from New Orleans to Cairo* (Chapel Hill, 1936). It told the story of three small lines that became a part of the Illinois Central. It was "A significant contribution . . . more than the story of a railroad," wrote the reviewer in the *Journal of Southern History*. The author had enlivened his subjects "with numerous bits of humor."[3]

The transplanted Mississippian soon saw the need for a modern one-volume history of Kentucky to replace the dated multivolumed sets. *A History of Kentucky* (Lexington, 1937) met that need. It was praised for "a clear readable style" and for Clark's attention to nonpolitical aspects of the state's history.[4] One reviewer suggested that Clark was more objective than most Kentuckians could have been.[5] A revised edition came out in 1950, and some changes were made later. The book has never gone out of print, and in some commonwealth homes it stands next to the King James version of the Bible. Clark has sometimes wished that he could do a multivolumed comprehensive history, but other projects have always interfered.

The frontier has been one of Clark's abiding interests, and in *The Rampaging Frontier: Manners and Humors of Pioneer Days in the South and Middle West* (Indianapolis, 1939) he penned one of his most readable books. It was "an exciting picture of that old frontier," but reviewer Carl Wittke added that "Some of this material will not please the fastidious, and is not intended for readers with weak stomachs." Then he added, "The book is entertaining and amusing on almost every page, but this should not blind the reader to the fact that it is a serious piece of historical craftsmanship, and a real contribution to American history and American humor."[6]

In the days before World War II, more Kentucky history was taught in public schools than is true today. Assisted by educator Lee Kirkpatrick, Clark wrote *Exploring Kentucky* (New York, 1939) to meet the need for a modern text for younger students.

As he explored Kentucky's past, Clark encountered several old works that he thought should be made available to current readers. He began editing such books with William Littell's *Festoons of Fancy: Consisting of Compositions Amatory, Sentimental, and Humorous in Verse and Prose* (Lousiville, 1814) Kentucky Reprint I (Lexington, 1940). Reprint II (Lexington, 1942) was John Magill's *The Pioneer to the Kentucky Emigrant: A Brief Topographical & Historical Description of the State of Kentucky to Which Are Added Some Original Verses* (Frankfort, 1932). Kentucky Reprint III (Lexington, 1945) was Harry Toulmin's *A Description of Kentucky in North America: To Which Are Prefixed Miscellaneous Observations Respecting the United States* (London, 1793). This reprint received more praise than the first two, and the reviewer in the *American Historical Review* commented that it was "another example of the good work which Professor Clark has been doing in collecting and republishing rare Americana."[7]

The American River Series had attracted favorable attention, and Clark was delighted with an invitation to contribute *The Kentucky*

(New York, 1942) to the series. A state review called it "pleasing, informative and scholarly. It is easy to read and the reader, at the end, is glad that he has read."[8] Another review called it "a readable account of the social life of the Kentucky country" and commented that the author had "gathered much of the material for this book at the sources."[9] A Bicentennial Edition (Lexington, 1992) included a new chapter that brought the story of the river up to date.

During the decade of the 1940s, Clark, by then head of the Department of History at the University of Kentucky, published two of his most important and favorite works. Both *Pills, Petticoats, and Plows: The Southern Country Store* (Indianapolis, 1944) and *The Southern Country Editor* (Indianapolis, 1948) were based on his extensive research throughout the South. The records that he brought back to Lexington were major additions to the University of Kentucky archives. William H. Hesseltine wrote of the former that "Professor Clark has told its story in a style that fits the subject—with a wealth of anecdote, a ready wit, and an insight into the human values concerned."[10] Clark's pioneering examination of these two major regional institutions revealed a number of areas in which research needed to be done. He had hoped to complete a trilogy with *The Southern Country School,* but the topic was preempted before he got to it. These two studies are major contributions to the historical profession—and to general readers.

In his study of early Kentucky, Clark had been impressed by the exploits of Simon Kenton, whose woodsman skills matched those of his friend, Daniel Boone. To provide reading suitable for young readers, Clark wrote *Simon Kenton, Kentucky Scout* (New York, 1943). The Jesse Stuart Foundation reprinted it in 1993. To encourage student research, he wrote *Kentucky: A Student's Guide to Localized History* (New York, 1955) for the Localized History Series, a project at Teachers College, Columbia University. He also became involved with collaborators in the production of two books aimed largely at juvenile readers. Together with Ray Compton and Amber Wilson he wrote *America's Frontier* (Chicago, 1958), and he and Daniel J. Beeby published *America's Old World Frontiers* (Chicago, 1962). In 1959 Clark wrote a short tribute to a former student who had drowned while trying to rescue a friend. *Harry V. McChesney III, 1935-1958* (privately printed, 1959) reflected Clark's lifetime concern for students.

Bluegrass Cavalcade (Lexington, 1956) was a collection of readings about the state and some of its most interesting characters and events. The editor included three of his own pieces, and few readers complained of dull reading. Three years later Clark published another book, *Frontier America: The Story of the Westward Movement* (New York, 1959). Both were well received by the reading public.

Clark had long used travel accounts as an essential part of his own research, and he decided that a bibliography of such accounts would be of great benefit to researchers in southern history. The University of Oklahoma Press was interested in the idea, and Clark agreed to edit a six-volume *Travels in the South* with specialists compiling the lists for each period. E. Merton Coulter had already worked on a list for the Civil War years, and his *Travels in the Confederate States: A Bibliography* (Norman, 1948) came out quickly. *Travels in the Old South*, Volume I, *The Formative Years, 1527-1831: From the Spanish Exploration through the American Revolution* (1956) followed, but the other two volumes were delayed until 1969. Volumes II, *The Expanding South: The Ohio Valley and the Cotton Frontier* (1969) and III, *The Ante Bellum South, 1825-1860: Cotton, Slavery and Conflict* (1969) completed that series. *Travels in the New South: A Bibliography* consisted of two volumes: I, *The Postwar South, 1865-1900: An Era of Reconstruction and Readjustment* (1962), and II, *The Twentieth Century South, 1900-1955: An Era of Change, Depression, and Emergence* (1962). Editor Clark did the section on "The New South, 1880-1900."

This extensive bibliography, recently reprinted, is one of his most important legacies to historians of the South.

In *The Emerging South* (New York, 1961), Clark examined the changes in the South between 1920 and 1960. A reviewer wrote that "much of *The Emerging South* is made up of chatty reports on the contemporary scene, mingled with gentle sermons about present and future needs." While the author generally avoided nostalgia, said the reviewer, it was obvious that he drew upon "a fullness of knowledge and personal contact with the subject."[11] Clark saw much that remained to be done in the South, but he praised the section for making some great changes, especially after World War II. He continued his examination of the recent South with *Three Paths to the Modern South: Education, Agriculture, and Conservation* (Athens, Ga., 1965), a series of lectures he gave at Mercer University in October 1964. Clark had become more interested in conservation (he owned forest lands in both Kentucky and South Carolina), and he stressed that factor. He and Albert D. Kirwan, a student and then colleague in the University of Kentucky history department, did a comprehensive survey of *The South since Appomattox: A Century of Regional Change* (New York, 1967). One reviewer praised the book for "its liberality and breadth of viewpoint," but a Kentucky reviewer protested that "the book gives an impression of dislike of the South."[12]

Clark's contribution to the Regions of America Series was *Kentucky: Land of Contrast* (New York, 1968). His descriptions of the several Kentuckys were "well written with a certain light-hearted charm that is a Clark trademark," according to the *Journal of Southern History* critic. The reviewer for a state journal complained that too much attention was paid to the Bluegrass region, but then admitted that "combining the talent of the storyteller with the wisdom of the social critic, he brings to life the struggles, joys, and sorrows, virtues, and short-comings of Old Kentucky."[13]

The reconstruction of the Shaker community at Pleasant Hill near Lexington had fascinated Clark, and with F. Gerald Ham he wrote *Pleasant Hill and Its Shakers* (Pleasant Hill, 1968), a handsome volume published by the Shakertown Press. It was a good introduction to one of the more interesting religious sects of the nineteenth century. The community never fully recovered from its Civil War trials, and Clark described its problems in *Pleasant Hill in the Civil War* (Shakertown, 1972).

In the late 1960s Clark edited another frontier account, but this time he went farther west with *Gold Rush Diary: Being the Journal of Elisha Douglass Perkins on the Overland Trail in the Spring and Summer of 1849* (Lexington, 1967). The editor used copious notes from other sources to enrich this account. The next year Holman Hamilton, once a student of Clark's, then a colleague and friend, edited *Three American Frontiers: Writings of Thomas D. Clark* (Lexington, 1968). Hamilton divided his selections into three groups: The Frontier West and South; The Frontier of Social Change; and The Frontier of Historical Research. In his favorable review of "a very useful book," Gilbert Fite commented that "There was scarcely any phase of the historical profession where his mark cannot be found."[14]

Although he was listed only as an associate editor of *Kentucky: A Pictorial History* (Lexington, 1971), he had a major role in fostering the concept and in producing one of the best selling products of the University Press of Kentucky. Before the *Pictorial History* appeared, Clark was well embarked on the largest writing project of his career. Elvis Stahr, a former student of Clark's who was then president of Indiana University, asked him to accept an appointment as Distinguished Service Professor and to write a comprehensive history of IU. Clark spent the years 1968-73 in Bloomington. In addition to teaching and writing the institutional history, he was at that time executive secretary of the Organization of American Historians. Clark's four volumes of *Indiana University: Midwestern Pioneer* told the story of a small, struggling school that became a major national institution. While the author did not say so, it was evident that IU had attained a status that had eluded UK. *The Early Years* (Bloomington, 1970), *In Mid-Passage* (1973), and *Years of Fulfillment* (1977) carried the story to the mid-1970s. *Historical Documents since 1816* (1977) brought the total pages in the project to over 2,200. It received almost universal praise. Merle Curti judged it "unexcelled in the historiography of American higher education." It was "hard to think of any way this book could have been better." Another reviewer echoed his assessment: "this study will take its place as one of the truly superior histories of an American institution of higher learning."[15]

The IU history highlighted Clark's writings in the 1970s, one of his most productive decades. *Helm Bruce, Public Defender: Breaking Louisville's Gothic Political Ring, 1905* (Louisville, 1973) related the story of an urban reformer who had some success in the state's largest city. Two other books appeared the same year. Clark edited *The South since Reconstruction* (Indianapolis, 1973). Its sixty-two selections centered on race relations and the economy, the themes Clark considered most important. The South had made much progress, Clark said, but too many Southerners continued to cling to tradition and myth. His twenty-five page introduction was a good overview of the period. He also edited *South Carolina: The Grand Tour, 1780-1865* (Columbia, S.C., 1973), a selection of travel accounts of persons who visited the state during that period.

Clark never strayed far from the frontier, and he returned to it with an edition of readings, *The Great American Frontier: A Story of Western Pioneering* (Indianapolis, 1975). It was followed by *Off at Sunrise: The Overland Journal of Charles Glass Gray* (San Marino, Cal., 1976). Clark was praised for the quality of his editing, including a fine bibliography.

Toward the end of the decade, Clark returned to a Kentucky topic in *Agrarian Kentucky* (Lexington, 1977), one of the forty-seven volumes in the Bicentennial Bookshelf issued by the University Press of Kentucky. Clark had played a major role in the development of this project and in securing backing for it. Restricted by the compact size of the books, which were aimed at the general reader, he provided an overview of one of his favorite subjects, and he indicated a number of topics that needed more study. He also edited a collection of twelve essays, most of them presented at the Ohio-Indiana spring conference of the American Studies Association, in *Onward and Upward: Essays on the Self-made American* (Bowling Green, Oh., 1979). Clark closed the decade with *Historic Maps of Kentucky* (Lexington, 1979), a valuable selection of early maps, some of them quite rare, with his text. The research required considerable field work to locate ancient markers, and Clark, well into his seventies, walked some much younger editors into a frazzle.

Tom Clark had always encouraged the writing of good local history, but he disliked antiquarianism. In the 1980s he made some contributions to the local history genre. *A Century of Banking History in the Bluegrass: The Second National Bank and Trust Company of Lexington, Kentucky* (Lexington, 1983) placed that fiscal institution in the context of state and national developments. Then for the Laurel County Historical Society he wrote *A History of Laurel County* (London, Ky., 1989). That story was also well told in the context of state and national history, and reviewer Robert M. Ireland called it "a richly woven narrative." He hoped that "Clark's study will encourage professional historians to write detailed histories of some of the other counties of Kentucky."[16]

Other works appearing during the decade saw Clark returning to some of his favorite subjects. For the New Perspectives on the South series he wrote *The Greening of the South: The Recovery of Land and*

Forest (Lexington, 1984). One reviewer commented that it had the insight of a tree farmer who had the "knack for coming up with the right phrase," but he objected to the lack of footnotes and thought that some terms needed to be defined for the general reader.[17] *Footloose in Jacksonian America: Robert W. Scott and His Agrarian World* (Frankfort, 1989) traced the visits of a Kentucky agrarian to parts of the United States. It told something about the nature of Jacksonian democracy as he saw it. Praised for its "pleasant, rambling style," a reviewer complained that some recent sources on that period had not been used.[18] With John D.W. Guise, Clark returned to one of his favorite areas with *Frontiers in Conflict: The Old Southwest, 1795-1830* (Albuquerque, N.M., 1989). It was generally called a good synthesis of developments in that region in its pioneer stage.

In the early 1990s Clark again had a significant role in the publication of another major project of the University Press of Kentucky. He pushed the concept of a comprehensive encyclopedia for the state, helped arrange financing, served as an associate editor, and contributed a large number of entries. He also wrote the overview introduction to two centuries of Kentucky statehood. Inevitably there were complaints about some omissions and the absence of illustrations, but *The Kentucky Encyclopedia* (Lexington, 1992) was a great success.

John Bradford, editor of the *Kentucky Gazette* in its early days, wrote a series of sixty-six articles for the paper in 1822-29 that were based in part on his personal knowledge of men and events in the pioneer era. Few general readers had access to the files of the *Gazette*, and Clark edited *The Voice of the Frontier: John Bradford's Notes on Kentucky* (Lexington, 1993). He followed that well-received work by helping edit *Kentucky's Historic Farms: 200 Years of Kentucky Agriculture* (Paducah, 1994), and wrote the introductory overview for the book. Clark probably has no idea of the number of prefaces, introductions, and overviews he has produced. Assisted by the Clark

County–Winchester Heritage Commission and the Clark County Historical Society, Clark penned *Clark County, Kentucky* (Winchester, 1996). (No, the county was named for George Rogers Clark, not Thomas D. Clark.) While reviewer John E.L. Robertson blamed the press, the editors, the sponsors, and the author for errors that should have been corrected, he also praised the scope of the work and the author's "deep and abiding empathy for the land."[19] Clark closed the decade with lovely coffee-table productions together with photographer James Archambeault. *Kentucky I* (Portland, Ore., 1982), *Kentucky II* (Portland, Ore., 1989), and *Kentucky III* (Portland, Ore., 1999) were all written by Clark.

Tom Clark's first work of the twenty-first century, done with Margaret A. Lane, was *The People's House: Governor's Mansions of Kentucky* (Lexington, 2002). Lavishly illustrated with many rare images, it relates the story of the buildings that have housed most of the state's governors and some of the interesting people who have lived in them.

As one examines the long list of books that Thomas D. Clark has authored and edited, one has to be impressed by both the quantity and the quality of his work. Of course some books turn out better than others, but he has maintained a consistently high quality throughout his long career. While they have been praised over the years by fellow historians, they have also been read and enjoyed by generations of appreciative general readers. The amazing quantity is explained in part by his remarkable creative longevity; much can be accomplished in seventy years. But even more important is the fact that Clark has worked consistently at his writing. He has never spent long hours in a faculty lounge complaining that he never had time to do his seminal project. His books testify to his success.

Even with his productive output over so many years, there are subjects that Tom Clark wishes he had written on. So much could have been included in a multivolumed history of Kentucky. He once planned to do a biography of John Fox Jr., but access to the Fox papers was denied. He also thought of writing biographies of George D. Prentice, the able editor of the *Louisville Journal*, or of Governor A.O. Stanley. And a book on the southern country school would have completed a trilogy on three important southern institutions.

Clark has never singled out the one book that is his favorite among the many he has produced; perhaps it is impossible for him to do so. But if pushed he will mention several works for which he has particular fondness.[20] *A History of Kentucky* is on that short list, along with *Pills, Petticoats, and Plows* and *The Southern Country Editor*. *The Kentucky, Frontier America*, and *Kentucky: Land of Contrast* are titles that many of his readers would insist that he include. *Travels in the South* was a major contribution to the historical profession, and the history of Indiana University represented some of his finest writing.

ARTICLES: A SELECT LIST

It would be almost impossible to list all of Clark's articles and chapters in books, for he has contributed essays to a wide variety of publications, many of which do not show up in scholarly listings. This prolific output is due in part to his concern for and interest in local history. This select list, confined largely to articles that appeared in historical publications, reveals his interest in several fields. They are presented in chronological order.

"The Ante-bellum Hemp Trade of Kentucky with the Cotton Belt." *Register* 27 (May 1929): 538-44.
"The Lexington and Ohio Railroad—A Pioneer Venture." *Register* 31 (Jan. 1933): 9-28.
"The Montgomery and West Point Railroad Company." *Georgia Historical Quarterly* 17 (Dec. 1933): 293-98.

"The Slave Trade between Kentucky and the Cotton Kingdom." *MVHR* 21 (Dec. 1934): 331-42.

"The Development of the Nashville and Chattanooga Railroad." *Tennessee Historical Magazine*, ser. 2, vol. 3 (April 1935): 160-68.

"The Slavery Background of Foster's 'My Old Kentucky Home.'" *FCHQ* 10 (Jan. 1936): 1-17.

"The Building of the Memphis and Charleston Railroad." *East Tennessee Historical Society Publications* 8 (1936): 9-25.

"Salt: A Factor in the Settlement of Kentucky." *FCHQ* 12 (Jan. 1938): 42-52.

"The People, William Goebel, and the Kentucky Railroads." *JSH* 5 (Feb. 1939): 34-48.

"Manners and Humors of the American Frontier." *Missouri Historical Review* 35 (Oct. 1940): 3-24.

"Traveler's Accounts as a Source of Kentucky History." *FCHQ* 14 (Oct. 1940): 205-23.

"Kentucky Heritage." In H.W. Beers, ed., *Kentucky: Designs for Her Future* (Lexington, 1945), 8-33.

"The Furnishing and Supply System in Southern Agriculture since 1865." *JSH* 12 (Feb. 1946): 24-44.

"The American Backwoodsman in Popular Portraiture." *IMH* 42 (March 1946): 1-28.

"My Old Kentucky Home in Retrospect." *FCHQ* 22 (April 1948): 104-16.

"The Background to Kentucky History: The Eighteenth and Nineteenth Centuries." *Register* 46 (Oct. 1948): 628-36.

"The Country Newspaper: A Factor in Southern Opinion, 1865-1930." *JSH* 14 (Feb. 1948): 3-33.

"The Rural South: The Country Store and the Rural Weekly." *Mississippi Quarterly* 2 (Dec. 1949): 1-7.

"The Archives of a Small Business." *American Archivist* 12 (Jan. 1949): 27-35.

"The Tennessee Country Editor." *East Tennessee Historical Society Publications* 21 (1949): 3-8.

"Research Possibilities in Southern History." *JSH* 16 (Feb. 1950): 52-63.

"The County Store in American Social History." *Ohio State Archaeological and Historical Quarterly* 60 (April 1951): 126-44.

"My Name Is Charles Guiteau." *AH* 2 (Summer 1951): 14-17, 69.

"The Country Newspaper as a Source of Social History." *IMH* 48 (Sept. 1952): 217-32.

"Virgins, Villains and Varmints: Beedle's Dime Novels." *AH* 3 (Spring 1952): 42-46.

"The Preservation of Southern Historical Documents." *American Archivist* 16 (Jan. 1953): 27-37.

"The Common Man Tradition in the Literature of the Frontier." *Michigan Alumnus Quarterly Review* 43 (May 1957): 208-17.

"The Great Visitation to American Democracy." *MVHR* 44 (June 1957): 3-28.

"The Modern South in a Changing America." *Proceedings of the American Philosophical Society* 107 (April 1963): 121-31.

"The Mississippi River in History." *Mississippi Quarterly* 16 (Fall 1963): 181-90.

"American Indians and Pioneers before and after James Fenimore Cooper." *Fort Wayne Ind. Public Library* (1968): 1-24.

"Wendell Holmes Stephenson, 1899-1970: Master Editor and Teacher." *JSH* 36 (Aug. 1970): 335-49.

"The Changing Emphases in the Writing of Southern History." *FCHQ* 45 (April 1971): 145-57.

"The Piedmont South in Historical Perspective." *Mississippi Quarterly* 24 (Winter 1971): 1-17.

"The Impact of the Timber Industry on the South." *Mississippi Quarterly* 25 (Spring 1972): 141-64.

"Boonesborough—Outpost of the American Westward Movement." *Register* 72 (Oct. 1974): 391-97.

"State and Local History: The Bedrock of Our Past." *East Tennessee Historical Society Publications* 48 (1976): 3-20.

"The Jackson Purchase: A Dramatic Chapter in Southern Indian Policy and Relations." *FCHQ* 50 (July 1976): 302-20.

"Our Roots Flourished in the Valley." *JAH* 65 (June 1978): 85-107.

"Sports on the Kentucky Frontier." In Humber S. Nelli, ed., *Sports in Society: Past and Present* (Lexington, 1980): 7-13.

"Ashland: The Home of Henry Clay." In Elisabeth Garrett, comp., *The Antiques Book of Victorian Interiors* (New York, 1981), 16-21.

"Clement Eaton." *Register* 80 (Spring 1982): 140-50.

"Reuben T. Durrett and His Kentuckiana Interest and Collection." FCHQ 56 (Oct. 1982): 353-78.

"Holman Hamilton." In James C. Klotter and Peter Sehlinger, eds., *Kentucky Profiles: Biographical Essays in Honor of Holman Hamilton* (Frankfort, 1982), 1-10. [Clark also wrote the Introduction.]

"Rogers Clark Ballard Thruston: Engineer, Historian and Benevolent Kentuckian." *FCHQ* 58 (Oct. 1984): 408-35.

"Kentucky Education through Two Centuries of Political and Social Change." *Register* 83 (Summer 1985): 173-201.

"The Kentucky Heritage: An Overview." *FCHQ* 66 (July 1992): 305-33.

"Constitution Making in Kentucky in Retrospect." *Kentucky Bench and Bar* 56 (Winter 1992): 1-22.

"Harry Caudill, Native Son." *Appalachian Heritage* 21 (Spring 1993): 1-14.

Bibliographical Works

The most comprehensive survey of Clark's life and work is Bill Cunningham, *Kentucky's Clark* (Kuttawa, Ky., 1987). It has a sketch of Clark's life (pp. 5-14) and an outline of his career (pp. 174-78); the rest of the book consists of Cunningham's questions and Clark's responses on a wide variety of topics. It also includes sixteen pages of photographs.

Professors Frank Steely and H. Lew Wallace of Northern Kentucky University did three interviews with Clark in the summer of 1982. Their "Thomas D. Clark: A Biographical Sketch," appeared in the *Filson Club History Quarterly* 60 (July 1986): 293-318. "An Interview with Thomas D. Clark" and "The Work of Thomas D. Clark: A Select Bibliography" appeared in *Plantation Society in the Americas* 3 (Summer 1996): 236-308, 309-20.

In his introduction to *Three American Frontiers: The Writings of Thomas D. Clark*, editor Holman Hamilton describes the career of his mentor. Roger Adelson, "Interview with Thomas D. Clark," *The Historian* 54 (Spring 1992): 411-24, and George Yater, "Interview with Dr. Thomas Clark, Historian, Teacher and Kentucky Author," *Louisville Magazine* 27 (July 1976): 79-88, provide essential information but do not discuss his writings in detail. Many brief sketches of Clark's career have appeared in other sources.

Clark has published two autobiographical essays: "Growing up with the Frontier," *Western Historical Quarterly* 3 (Oct. 1972): 360-72, and "Recollections of a Mississippi Boyhood," in Dorothy Abbott, ed., *Mississippi Writers: Reflections of Childhood and Youth*, 3 vols. (Jackson, Miss., 1986) 2: 114-24.

NOTES

1. Bill Cunningham, *Kentucky's Clark* (Kuttawa, Ky., 1987), 120.
2. Ibid., 146.
3. *JSH* 3 (May 1937): 229-30.
4. *JSH* 4 (Feb. 1938): 98-99.
5. *FCHQ* 11 (Oct. 1937): 275.
6. *JSH* 5 (Aug. 1939): 399.
7. *AHR* 51 (July 1946): 777.
8. *FCHQ* 16 (July 1942): 198.
9. *JSH* 8 (Aug. 1942): 434-35.
10. *MVHR* 31 (Sept. 1944): 281.
11. *JSH* 28 (Nov. 1962): 522.
12. *JSH* 33 (Aug. 1967): 377; Janet Lowell Walker, *FCHQ* 41 (July 1967): 280.
13. *JSH* 34 (Nov. 1968): 642; *FCHQ* 42 (Oct. 1968): 351-52.
14. *JAH* 56 (Dec. 1968): 643.
15. *AHR* 83 (Oct. 1978): 1101; *JAH* 65 (Dec. 1978): 836-37.
16. *FCHQ* 64 (Oct. 1994): 506-7.
17. *JAH* 72 (March 1986): 974.
18. *JAH* 78 (Sept. 1991): 659.
19. *Register* 95 (Winter 1997): 86-88.
20. Thomas D. Clark to Lowell H. Harrison, Oct. 11, 2002.

Contributors

NANCY DISHER BAIRD, Special Collections Librarian at Western Kentucky University, has taught Kentucky history as well as written about many aspects of the commonwealth's past. She currently serves as Interim Department Head for Western's Kentucky Library and Museum.

WALTER A. BAKER is an attorney in Glasgow, Kentucky, and President of the Kentucky Historical Society. Baker is a graduate of Harvard College and Harvard Law School and served over two decades in the Kentucky General Assembly, first as a State Representative, then for several terms as a State Senator. He is also a former justice of the Kentucky Supreme Court.

JAMES DUANE BOLIN is a professor of history at Murray State University, where he teaches courses in American History, Sports History, Kentucky History, and Teaching History. In 2000, he published *Bossism and Reform in a Southern City: Lexington, Kentucky, 1880-1940,* and *Kentucky Baptists, 1925-2000: A Story of Cooperation.* Bolin graduated magna cum laude from Belmont University in Nashville, TN. After a year of graduate study and a period of teaching in Kentucky public schools, he completed a master's degree and a Ph.D. in history at the University of Kentucky. He has taught at several institutions, and has been awarded several Faculty Member of the Year awards. Bolin lives in Murray, Kentucky, with his wife, Evelyn, and their children.

CAROL CROWE CARRACO, Distinguished University Professor of History at Western Kentucky University, has taught, written, and lectured widely on state, local, and Kentucky history. Dr. Carraco established the women's studies program at WKU.

EDWARD M. COFFMAN was born and educated in Hopkinsville and did all of his undergraduate and graduate work at the University of Kentucky. In addition to teaching at Memphis State University (now University of

Memphis) and the University of Wisconsin-Madison, he served as a visiting professor at Kansas State University, West Point, the Air Force Academy, the Army Command and General Staff College, and the Army War College. He has published three books—*The Hilt of the Sword: The Career of Peyton C. March, The War to End All Wars: The American Military Experience in World War I,* and *The Old Army: A Portrait of the American Army in Peacetime, 1784–1898.* After retirement from the University of Wisconsin, he and his wife moved back to Lexington.

WM. JEROME CROUCH is a native of Georgia, but grew up in Arkansas. He attended high school and college at Berea, received his bachelor's degree at the University of Arizona and his master's degree in English at the University of Kentucky. Along the way he mapped county roads for the Arkansas State Highway Department, taught English composition at Augustana (Illinois) College, and served as a traveler in the South for the college department of the Macmillan Company before joining the University of Kentucky Press as a editor in 1962. During his time at the Press he was privileged to work with Thomas D. Clark on the publication of *Gold Rush Diary* and on the reissue of *The Kentucky.* He retired from the Press in 1993.

LEONARD P. CURRY was born in Cave City, Kentucky, in 1929. He took undergraduate degrees from Campbellsville College and Western Kentucky State College (BA, 1951). After a short period of service in the U.S. Air Force he earned a master's (1956) and a Ph.D. (1961) from the University of Kentucky. He taught at Memphis State University from 1958 to 1962, then joined the faculty of the University of Louisville, where he taught until his retirement in 1999, at which time he was chair of the history department. He also served as visiting assistant professor at the University of Maine, Orono, and as visiting associate professor at the University of Maryland, College Park. He is author of *Blueprint for Modern America: Nonmilitary Legislation of the First Civil War Congress* (Vanderbilt, 1968); *Rail Routes South: Louisville's Struggle for the Southern Market* (Kentucky, 1969); *The Free Black in Urban America, 1800–1850: The Shadow of the Dream* (Chicago, 1981); and *The Corporate City: The American City as a Political Entity, 1800–1850* (Greenwood, 1997), volume one of *The Emergence of American Urbanism, 1800–1850.*

CARL N. DEGLER was educated in the public schools of Newark, New

Jersey, and graduated from Upsala College (East Orange, New Jersey) with a B.A. in history in 1942. He served in the United States Army Air Force from 1942 through 1945, then earned an M.A. (1947) and a Ph.D. (1952) in American history from Columbia University. He taught at Hunter College, City College of New York, Adelphi University, New York University, and Vassar College. He was visiting professor at Columbia University Graduate School (1963-64) and Harold Vyvyan Harmsworth Professor of American History at Oxford University (1973-74). After 1968 he served as professor of history at Stanford University and was Margaret Byrne Professor of American History (1972-90). He is the author of seventy-five articles, more than one hundred reviews, and many books, one of which, *Neither Black Nor White,* won the Pulitzer Prize in History in 1972, the Bancroft Prize of Columbia University, and the Beveridge Prize of the American Historical Association. His book *In Search of Human Nature* was awarded the Ralph Waldo Emerson Prize by Phi Beta Kappa in 1991. He holds honorary degrees from Oxford University, Colgate University, Ripon College, and his alma mater Upsala College.

WILLIAM E. ELLIS is a graduate of Georgetown College, Eastern Kentucky University, and the University of Kentucky. He retired in 1999 at EKU after a total of thirty-six years teaching high school, junior college, and university students. His honors include a Fulbright to New Zealand in 1989, the Governor's Award in 1999 for *Robert Worth Bingham and the Southern Mystique,* and a Foundation Professorship at EKU. He is author of four histories, over thirty articles, and two books of fiction. His most recent book is *The Kentucky River.* He now serves as University Historian at EKU and is writing a centennial history of that school. He is also adjunct professor of history at The Baptist Seminary of Kentucky.

WADE HALL, a native of Union Springs, Alabama, has lived since 1962 in Louisville, where he has taught English and chaired the English and humanitites/arts programs at Kentucky Southern College and Bellarmine University. He has also taught at the University of Illinois and the University of Florida. He holds degrees from Troy State University (B.S.), the University of Alabama (M.A.), and the University of Illinois (Ph.D.). He served for two years in the U.S. Army in the mid-fifties. He is the author of books, monographs, articles, plays, and reviews relating to Kentucky, Alabama, and Southern history and literature. His most recent books include *A Visit with*

Harlan Hubbard; High Upon a Hill: A History of Bellarmine College; A Song in Native Pastures: Randy Atcher's Life in Country Music; and *Waters of Life from Conecuh Ridge.*

MARY WILMA HARGREAVES attended Bucknell University (AB, 1935), Radcliff College/Harvard University (M.A. 1936, Ph.D. 1951, history), and was a junior fellow at the Brookings Institution (1939-40). She is author of numerous articles and books, including *Dry Farming in the Northern Great Plains, 1900-1925* (Harvard, 1957), *Dry Farming in the Northern Great Plains, Readjustment Years, 1920-1990* (Kansas, 1993), and *Presidency of John Quincy Adams* (Kansas, 1985), and is associate editor/coeditor of *Papers of Henry Clay,* volumes I through VI (Kentucky, 1959-81).

LOWELL HARRISON was a combat engineer in Europe during WWII. He graduated (A.B.) from Western Kentucky in 1946 and earned his M.A. (1947) and Ph.D. (1951) from New York University. He taught at NYU briefly, at West Texas State University from 1952-1967, and at Western Kentucky from 1967 until his retirement in 1988. He is the author of numerous articles and books, including *Lincoln of Kentucky, The Civil War in Kentucky, Kentucky's Road to Statehood, George Rogers Clark and the War in the West, Western Kentucky University,* and *The Antislavery Movement in Kentucky,* and is co-author of *A New History of Kentucky.*

JOHN E. KLEBER was born in Louisville, Kentucky. He graduated summa cum laude from Bellarmine University (1963) and received two graduate degrees from the University of Kentucky (M.A., 1965; Ph.D. 1969). He did post-graduate study at the University of California, Ivine. He began as an assistant professor of history at Morehead State University in 1968, and retired in May 1996 as professor emeritus. He served as director of the Academic Honors Program (1973–88) and interim dean of the Caudill College of Humanities (1993–95). He received the Outstanding Civil Service Medal (1971) from the U.S. Army, the Outstanding Teacher Award (1982) and Distinguished Researcher Award (1993) from Morehead State, the Catholic Alumni Award (2002) from the Archdiocese of Louisville, the Governor's Outstanding Kentuckian Award (1992), and is a distinguished alumnus of Trinity High School and Bellarmine University. He was a member of the Kentucky Oral History Commission (1981-92) and the Kentucky Humanities Council Board (1996-2001). He also served as a visiting professor of history at the University of Louisville. He is the editor of *The Public Papers of Lawrence W. Wetherby* (1983), *The Kentucky Encyclopedia* (1992), and *The Encyclopedia of Louisville* (2001). He spoke before the Kentucky State Senate at the opening of the General Assembly January 1998 on the state of Kentucky at century's end. He was named to the Mayor's Millennium Commission, and he chaired its Historic Preservation committee. He resides in Jefferson County.

JAMES C. KLOTTER, a native Kentuckian, received his Ph.D. in history from the University of Kentucky. He is the author, coauthor, or editor of more than a dozen books, including *A New History of Kentucky* (with Lowell H. Harrison) and *Kentucky: Portrait in Paradox, 1900-1950*. Dr. Klotter was formerly the Executive Director of the Kentucky Historical Society and is now professor of history at Georgetown College and the State Historian of Kentucky.

WILLIAM MARSHALL, archivist and baseball historian, has served as Director of Special Collection and Archives at the University of Kentucky since 1976 and is author of *Baseball's Pivotal Era, 1945-1951*. He is particularly indebted to Dr. Clark for his efforts in preserving history at the University and has attempted to continue that legacy.

JOHN ED PEARCE was born in Norton, Virginia, in 1919. He graduated from the Norton public schools and attended the University of Kentucky. He has been at the forefront of Kentucky journalism for the past sixty years. After Navy service in World War II, he edited the *Somerset* (Ky.) *Journal* briefly before joining *The Courier-Journal* of Louisville in 1946, where for fifty years he served as editorial writer, associate editor, magazine writer, and columnist. He became a columnist for the Lexington Herald-Leader in 1993, a post he still holds. In his career he shared in the Pulitzer Prise, has been awarded a Nieman Fellowship to Harvard, a Headliner Award, a Meeman Award for Conservation, three Silver Gavel Awards, and a Genesis Award. He was named Outstanding Kentucky Journalist by Sigma Delta Chi and was named to the University of Kentucky Journalism Hall of Fame. In 1966 he was awarded the Governor's Medallion for Public Service. He is a Commander in the U.S. Navy Reserve, served in World War II and Vietnam, and was a group leader at the National War College. He is the author of nine books, dozens of magazine articles, television plays, and two television documentaries. He is the father of five daughters. He divides his time among Louisville, Lexington, and Upper Captiva Island, Florida.

CHARLES P. ROLAND is an emeritus Alumni Professor of History at the University of Kentucky. A native of Tennessee, he hold the B.A. degree from Vanderbilt University and the M.A. and Ph.D. degrees from Louisiana State University. He has served on the faculty of Tulane University and as the visiting professor of military history at the U.S. Army Military History Institute and Army War College and at the U.S. Military Academy at West Point. He is the author of many books and articles on the South and on the Civil War. He is a former president of the Southern Historical Association. He lives in Lexington, Kentucky, with his wife, Allie Lee.

ROBERT F. SEXTON has been executive director of the Prichard Committee for Academic Excellence, an independent, state-wide, non-partisan advocacy group dedicated to the improvement of education for all Kentuckians, since its creation in 1983. He has, in fact, been involved in public education reform at both a local and a national level, and has been recognized for his efforts by receiving honorary degrees from several institutions, as well as the Charles A. Dana award for Pioneering Achievement. Dr. Sexton graduated from Yale University and received a Ph.D. in history from the University of Washington. He was a Visiting Scholar at Harvard University and at the Annanberg Institute for School Reform at Brown University, and founded Kentucky's Governor's Scholars Program and the Commonwealth Institute for Teachers. He lives in Lexington with his wife Pam, and has five grown children.

Index